Politics and Progress

Politics and Progress

The Emergence of American Political Science

Dennis J. Mahoney

Foreword by Harry V. Jaffa

LEXINGTON BOOKS
Lanham • Boulder • New York • Toronto • Oxford

LEXINGTON BOOKS

Published in the United States of America
by Lexington Books
An imprint of The Rowman & Littlefield Publishing Group, Inc.
4501 Forbes Boulevard, Suite 200, Lanham, Maryland 20706

PO Box 317
Oxford
OX2 9RU, UK

British Library Cataloguing in Publication Information Available

Library of Congress Cataloging-in-Publication Data

Mahoney, Dennis J.
  Politics and progress : the emergence of American political science /
Dennis J. Mahoney.
      p. cm.
Includes bibliographical references (p.   ) and index.
  ISBN 0-7391-0655-4 (cloth : alk. paper) — ISBN 0-7391-0656-2 (pbk. :
alk. paper)
  1. Political science—United States. 2. Political science. I. Title.

JA84.U5M26 2004
320'.0973—dc22   2003021079

Printed in the United States of America

⊖™ The paper used in this publication meets the minimum requirements of American
National Standard for Information Sciences—Permanence of Paper for Printed Library
Materials, ANSI/NISO Z39.48–1992.

To the memory of my mother,

Betty Jean Hutson Mahoney

(1923–2003)

CONTENTS

FOREWORD

Leo Strauss began *Natural Right and History*, first published in 1953, by quoting the passage of the Declaration of Independence, beginning, "We hold these truths to be self evident, that all men are created equal." "The nation dedicated to this proposition," Strauss continued,

> has now become, no doubt partly as a consequence of this dedication, the most powerful and prosperous of the nations of the earth. Does this nation, in its maturity, still cherish the faith in which it was conceived and raised? Does it still hold those "truths to be self-evident"?

A generation ago, Strauss said, an American diplomat could say that "the natural and divine foundation of the rights of man is self evident to all Americans." At about the same time

> a German scholar could still describe the difference between German thought and that of Western Europe and the United States by saying that the West still attached decisive importance to natural right, while in Germany the very terms "natural right" and "humanity" have become almost incomprehensible.

"While abandoning the idea of natural right and through abandoning it," he continued, "German thought has 'created the historical sense,'" and thus "was led eventually to unqualified relativism." Dennis Mahoney's work is the most precise account yet given of how German historical scholarship, and the "historical sense" as understood by that scholarship, came to inform and dominate the teaching of politics in American universities. In particular, it is an account of the intellectual influences that went into the formation of the American Political Science Association, exactly one hundred years ago. This was a major contributing cause in the transformation of American politics by the Progressive movement. As Mahoney shows, the necessary condition for the aforesaid transformation was the abandonment of "the laws of nature and of Nature's God" on the ground that History provided a philosophically and scientifically superior answer to questions of moral and political right and wrong. Yet, as Strauss proved, this "superior answer" was an assumption that was never proved to be true. Because the label of "science" has been pinned to it, it has taken the form of a prejudice so deeply engrained that the principles of the Declaration of Independence and of the Gettysburg Address are thought to be as obsolete as knights in armor, or sailing vessels. Nearly all the catastrophes of the twentieth century can, however, be traced, directly or indirectly, to the abandonment—here and abroad—of the natural right principles of the Founders and Lincoln.

The "unqualified relativism" which according to Strauss was the ultimate end of the historical sense was not however its immediate consequence. The belief in "progress' was a belief that political history was a branch of evolutionary history, and that it was a movement from the lower to the higher, an essentially involuntary movement that guaranteed moral as well as intellectual improvement in the human condition. The question of what ends were to be served by political science was a question that would not be answered by reasoning human beings but by history and which, therefore, did not have to be answered, or even considered, by political science. Political philosophy, as understood in the tradition of Plato and Aristotle, was no longer necessary.

Strauss spoke of a nation "dedicated" to a proposition. In speaking of the Declaration of Independence, Strauss used the language of Lincoln at Gettysburg. However, in *Lincoln at Gettysburg*, Garry Wills—echoing the late Willmoore Kendall—called the Gettysburg Address a "giant swindle." Wills hastened to add that it was a good swindle, whereas Kendall (a loyal son of the Old South) had thought it a bad one. The alleged swindle was that the Gettysburg Address had given a prominence to the idea of equality which it had never before possessed. John C. Calhoun, however, in his denunciation of the proposition of equality as "the most false and dangerous of all political errors," had nonetheless conceded that it had had a nearly universal currency at the Founding. According to the greatest enemy of the Declaration, the "swindle" charge had no foundation in historical fact.

Calhoun's attack against the idea of equality—the core principle of the Declaration of Independence—was centered on the allegedly unhistorical character of the idea of the state of nature. However exotic the state of nature may have appeared to the historical school—or may appear today in the wake of the depredations of the historical school—it is as analytically necessary to the idea of equality as that the three angles of the triangle equal two right angles. We can say, on the basis of a commonsense observation that anyone can make at any time, that there is no difference between any normal adult human being, and any other such human being, which would make one evidently or naturally the ruler of the other. This compares with the evident difference in nature between any human being and any dog or horse. Such difference makes the human being by nature the ruler of the dog or horse. It is also clear that the perfection we ascribe to God gives Him the same superiority over humans that humans have over beasts. There is therefore no reason why some humans should claim the right to rule other humans, as if some were gods, and others were beasts. The only legitimate human government must rest upon the consent of rational beings, members of the species *homo sapiens*. Such beings can consent to be governed only by a government in which those who live under the law share in making the law they live under, and those who make the law live under the law that they make. Hence the idea of equality is the heart of legitimate government and of the rule of law, and will so remain as long as the evident difference subsists between man, beast, and God.

James Madison often remarked that "compact is the essence of all free government." This was what others have called the "social contract." It is an agreement of each with all and of all with each, that they shall live under a government of law. This is a government which will protect equally the natural rights, to life, liberty, property, and the pursuit of happiness, of each consenting member. Not historical fate, but reason, declares that the government of rational beings is legitimate only when it rests upon their consent, and that rational beings can be presumed to consent only to a government based upon the ground of human equality. Most governments in the long, melancholy history of man have rested, not upon consent, but upon force. Most such governments have rested upon myths—false opinions—about the superiority of some human beings to others, as if they belonged to different species. Lincoln lumped all such myths together as the "divine right of kings," as if the members of certain families differed from other human beings, the way the queen bee differs from the workers or drones in a bee hive. The historical school has denied the equality of the rights of man under the laws of nature. "Historical right" cannot distinguish legitimate from illegitimate government on the basis of the equal protection of the laws. It cannot do so, because it identifies the successful use of force, not the successful use of reason, as the ultimate arbiter of the rights of those under government. It was the historical school that first identified American slavery, not as a necessary evil, but as a positive good. It was the historical school which asserted Aryan superiority—the master race—as justification for the enslavement (and even the extermination) of non-Aryan human beings. It was the historical school which claimed for the proletariat—the master class—the right to destroy all private property, and hence all private rights, the very rights for which the rule of law came into existence. The insanity of cultural relativism, which infects our campuses today, is a denial that there is any basis in reason for distinguishing polities which embody the principle of human equality and the rule of law, and those which do not. While denying that all men are created equal, they insist that all cultures are equal. They are said to be equal because they say that reason is unable to pronounce anything just or unjust, good or bad, better or worse. Their only truth is that there is no truth. We are not told why this alleged truth should claim exemption for itself. The nihilism into which historicism has resolved itself makes us all heirs of the Cretan who declared that all Cretans are liars. Dennis Mahoney's book is of major importance in illuminating the dark downward road we have traveled, and points the way to retrace our steps upward toward the light.

Harry V. Jaffa

INTRODUCTION

In the final years of the nineteenth and the first years of the twentieth centuries, a new political science emerged in America. Its principal observable characteristics were that it was academic and professional. But the essential difference between the American tradition of political science and the new academic political science was that the former was based on an understanding of immutable principles—self-evident truths—about the nature of man and of the political things while the latter was based on a notion of evolutionary progress which denied the existence of such principles. Frank J. Goodnow, the founding president of the American Political Science Association (A.P.S.A.), made that clear in the opening paragraph of a book published in 1911:

> The tremendous changes in political and social conditions due to the adoption of improved means of transportation and to the establishment of the factory system have brought with them problems whose solution seems to be impossible under the principles of law which were regarded as both axiomatic and permanently enduring at the end of the nineteenth century. That law was permeated by the theories of social compact and natural right, which in their turn were based upon the conception that society was static rather than dynamic or progressive in character.[1]

1

The new political science, of which the A.P.S.A. was the organizational embodiment and within which Goodnow was an acknowledged leader, was based upon the conception that society was dynamic and progressive.

The authors of a standard, if partisan, history of the discipline have with good cause written that "most American political scientists are largely unfamiliar with the origins and early evolution of their discipline [and] despite—or more likely because of—this unfamiliarity, the profession is very much the product and prisoner of its past."[2] The unfamiliarity extends beyond the chronological details of who taught whom and where, and who succeeded whom as president of the A.P.S.A., and what books were published when. The practitioners of the new political science seem unaware of the tacit assumptions which underlie the discipline's methods and activities.

The bulk of the present work is concerned with the influences on that discipline in its earlier stages (and especially with three variants of the ideology of progress), with the earlier nonacademic American political science that the new discipline displaced, and with the characteristics of the discipline as it was practiced by early academic political scientists. The purpose of the work is to bring to light the ideological underpinnings of the discipline and to show how the ideology of progress shaped the thought and work of academic political science from the beginning. These themes are treated within the context of the early history of the discipline, and that early history is delimited by certain events: the appointment of John W. Burgess as professor of political science at Columbia University in 1876, the establishment of the Columbia School of Political Science in 1880, the founding of the American Political Science Association in 1903–1904, the inauguration of political scientist Woodrow Wilson as president of the United States in 1913, and American participation in the First World War I in 1917–1918.

The emergence of political science as an academic discipline roughly coincided with the "Progressive Era"—a time "[w]hen both 'left' and 'right' in America sung variants of a hymn to Progress and its consubstantial Science . . . when sceptics of Progress . . . could be regarded by social scientists as between fools and knaves,"[3] and when "two great themes ar[o]se to dominate American social thought: . . . Progress and the idea of a Science of Society."[4] The ideology of progress (together with the scientism that accompanied it) was not the property of any political "wing." The conservative version was advanced by Herbert

Spencer, William Graham Sumner, and John W. Burgess; the liberal version by John Dewey, Herbert D. Croly, and Woodrow Wilson.

The era commencing in the decade following the Civil War was also "a revolutionary turning point in the history of American higher education. The age of the college had passed, and the age of the university was dawning."[5] So much so that "[t]o the men who experienced it, the time around 1870 seemed to mark 'almost the Anno Domini of educational history' in the United States."[6] Seen in this context, then,

> the emergence of political science as an independent discipline was part of a wholesale transformation which occurred in American higher education during the concluding decades of the nineteenth, and the opening years of the twentieth[,] centuries. In almost every area of scholarship, graduate training was reconstructed along Teutonic and, to a lesser degree, Gallic, lines.[7]

The universities of continental Europe were the models consciously imitated by those responsible for the educational revolution: "[t]he university, hallowed, yet newly thriving on the Continent, could uniquely satisfy the social idealism, the personal ambition, and the prideful American urge to equal the best of European achievements."[8] The emergence of a new political science was no small part of this academic revolution.

The study of politics, of course, was never excluded from American colleges and universities. Professors and departments of political science, so called, were absent, but the study of political things underlay the whole curriculum. Politics was the subject of courses denominated history, literature, law, or moral philosophy.[9] It was not until 1857, however, that Columbia College appointed America's first professor of political science, Francis Lieber.[10] And it was not until 1880 that Lieber's successor, John W. Burgess, established a graduate school of political science at Columbia.[11]

The great national trauma, then only recently past, had brought political questions to the forefront of public consciousness. "The study of Constitutional Law and of American history had originally been vastly stimulated, in both secondary and higher education, by the Civil War,"[12] and, in response, between 1875 and 1904, American universities began to appoint professors of political science. The men they chose were those who had trained in the universities of Germany, or at Columbia or the Johns Hopkins University (where they studied under professors trained in Germany). Those two American schools produced the bulk of American doctors of philosophy in political science until the turn of the twentieth century. The former was dominated by Burgess and his disciples, the latter by the historian Herbert Baxter Adams and the economist Richard T. Ely.

The story of American academic political science necessarily begins with John W. Burgess, the principal figure in the transformation of American political science. In a sense he was a "transitional" figure who led his followers to the boundary of the new academic discipline, but never crossed over it himself. He was the figure through whom the influence of German academic political science—probably the primary academic influence on the new discipline—was transmitted; but Burgess was more or less immune to the other influences, progressive reformism and pragmatism. Burgess was the founder of the first graduate department of political science in the United States and the teacher of the first generation of professors of political science in the country; but, though still very much alive in 1903–1904, he was not actively involved in the founding of the American Political Science Association. Although he attended the preliminary meeting in Washington, D.C., in December 1902, called to discuss the founding of an American Society for Comparative Legislation, he apparently never even joined the A.P.S.A.[13]

Burgess remains a controversial figure, about whom one writer could say that he "did much to establish the respectability of political science [but] contributed little to what became its dominant techniques and concerns,"[14] who, "[f]or all his long tenure in the Chair of Political Science at Columbia[,] left no disciples and is spoken of by the present leaders of opinion in the political science profession with the respectful vagueness as to what were his actual views that well demonstrates his unshakeable position in prehistory."[15]

At about the same time, however, others wrote that "Burgess ranks not only as the 'father' of American political science, but among the truly great figures in its history. His aspirations for a scientific politics, grasp of scientific method, insistence upon broad interdisciplinary training, and concern with systematic theory set a standard rarely surpassed from his day to the present."[16] Still another writer, an intellectual historian, has attempted to reconcile these apparently opposite perceptions, by remarking that "Burgess himself . . . managed to dominate the field while, paradoxically, having almost no real influence and few devoted disciples."[17] In fact, Burgess's greatest contributions to the emergence of the new political science were the importation of the methods of the German historical school of political science into America and the establishment of political science as a field of graduate study. He thereby laid the foundation upon which others built.

Burgess told in his autobiography how he came to pursue a career in political science. As a young soldier in 1863,

> I found myself murmuring to myself: "is it not possible for man, a being of reason, created in the image of God, to solve the problems of his existence without recourse to the destructive means of physical violence?" And then I registered a vow in heaven that if a kind Providence would deliver me alive from the perils of the existing war, I would devote my life to teaching men how to live by reason and compromise instead of by bloodshed and destruction.[18]

After leaving the Army he sought training to prepare himself to fulfill his vow. He attended Amherst College in Massachusetts, but was disappointed. "At Amherst I did not find the instruction in history, political science and public law which I was seeking. It did not exist at that time anywhere in our country."[19]

He therefore formed the plan, ultimately thwarted by a bout with typhoid, of enrolling in Columbia Law School. That school was virtually the private operation of Theodore W. Dwight. But the trustees of the college having hired Francis Lieber as professor of constitutional history and public law, and President Barnard having found those subjects unnecessary in the curriculum of Columbia College,[20] Dwight had Lieber thrust upon him as an associate and colleague. Officially, Lieber was the professor of constitutional and public law in the Columbia Law School, while Dwight taught the bulk of the law school curriculum. That suited Burgess fine: "It was, however, Professor Lieber rather than Professor Dwight who attracted me to the Columbia Law School, since his subjects were more nearly in line with that I had proposed myself as my life's work.[21]

Burgess's attraction to Lieber, based on Lieber's writings on public law, showed that he was already under the German spell. In fact, the spell had first been cast over him by Amherst chemistry professor William S. Clark, who had studied abroad and "first brought to Amherst from the German universities some of the methods and results of the German investigators in natural science."[22] But it was not Lieber who was to indoctrinate Burgess in the methods and concerns of German political science. Credit or blame must be given, in the first instance, to George Bancroft. On the advice of a relative, Burgess wrote to the elderly historian, then serving as the American Ambassador to Prussia, for advice. "In less than a month I received a reply from Mr. Bancroft offering himself to guide my studies, and recommending that I come immediately to Germany . . ."[23]

And Burgess did go immediately to Germany. In a period of about two years he attended lectures and seminars at three German universities, Goettingen, Leipzig, and Berlin. He came into contact with, and was influenced by, the leading German academics of his time in the fields of history and politics, and, more to the point, perhaps, he watched the triumph of the newly united German empire over the French in the Franco-Prussian war. That victory was a kind of proof of the efficacy of the political science taught and practiced in Germany.

Burgess returned from Germany to become a professor of history at Amherst, but his ultimate aim was to found a graduate seminary on the German model. He experimented along those lines at Amherst, but the real opportunity came when he was called to the chair of political science at Columbia College. There he taught in both the undergraduate college and the law school even while planning for the creation of a novel institution, an American graduate school of the political sciences. In this cause he allied himself with those Columbia trustees who sought to remodel the institution as a great university on the German model. Appointed professor at Columbia in 1876, Burgess promoted his scheme for an American graduate school of political science on the German model. His ultimate success in that endeavor came only after four years of cajoling and politicking among the trustees, many of whom, like many of the alumni, were reluctant to abandon the collegiate tradition.

Burgess was originally appointed professor of Political Science and Constitutional Law at Columbia in May 1876.[24] The Graduate Faculty of Political Sciences, and with it the beginning of the modern Columbia University, came into being in 1880.[25] Burgess became dean of the new school and secured the appointment of his most promising students as his assistants. These were young men trained by Burgess himself who, in most cases, had gone on to do graduate work at European universities. The first three colleagues Burgess recruited were previously students under him at Amherst; when one of them died in 1883, he was replaced by yet another of the protégés Burgess had attracted at Amherst.

The Columbia graduate program was the first graduate program of political science in America. From it came the first professors of political science at dozens of American colleges and universities. From it also came the first organization of American political scientists, the American Academy of Political Science (founded as a kind of alumni association for the graduate school) and the first American political science journal, the *Political Science Quarterly*. Under Burgess's direction and sponsorship the young professors produced the first series of textbooks for use in college political science courses.

The *Political Science Quarterly* was established at Columbia in 1886, because of Columbia's commitment to scholarly publication. The *Quarterly* remained the preeminent disseminator of scholarly articles from the political science profession at least until the founding of the *American Political Science Review*, a quarter of a century later. The growing professionalism, homogeneity, and sophistication of the discipline may be traced in the successive volumes of that first journal, an integral part of Burgess's plan for the Columbia school.

The main characteristics of the Columbia school in the early days were: interdisciplinary approach; comparative analysis; training in research methods, including statistics; emphasis on legal forms and institutions. Lecturers in the school were expected to be diligent researchers and productive scholars, much like the Prussian professors under whom Burgess had studied as a graduate student.

Somit and Tannenhaus, Development, the party historians of the behavioralist school, characterized the place of the Columbia School of Political Sciences in the history of the discipline as follows:

> Burgess's school offered the first, and for many years the most ambitious, graduate program of political science in the United States. But beyond this, it did not evolve gradually. Although the period of gestation may have been long and painful, the School sprang almost fully formed at birth from the minds of Burgess and his young associates. The Columbia School of Political Science was the formative institution in the development of the discipline, since its program was the one that other universities consciously emulated or deliberately deviated from in setting up their own graduate work in political science. . . . In fine, when the School opened in the Fall of 1880, American political science as a learned discipline was born.[26]

About the time Burgess began teaching at Columbia, the Johns Hopkins University was founded at Baltimore. Johns Hopkins was the first successful graduate school in America built to the specifications of the European university. Founded in 1876 with the proceeds of a gift from Johns Hopkins, the university was organized and the faculty assembled by Daniel Coit Gilman. The success of Hopkins was significant because it was "the first American institution to be founded as a university and not as a college . . . with the needs of graduate work in mind."[27]

Although there was no department of political science in the original organization of the university, there was a joint seminar taught by two German-trained scholars: historian Herbert B. Adams and economist Richard T. Ely. The seminar met in a room in which the motto was prominently displayed: "History is past Politics and Politics present History."[28] From this seminar came the second major group of new American political scientists. The Johns Hopkins program produced many of the distinguished early leaders of the profession, such as Woodrow Wilson and Westel W. Willoughby.

So completely did the two universities dominate the discipline that Somit and Tannenhaus could write:

> The only American Ph.D. programs of consequence before the end of the nineteenth century, it is safe to say, were those at Columbia and Johns Hopkins. Seventeen persons holding American doctorates were nominated for office or committee appointment at the first (1903) meeting of the American Political Science Association; of this group, seven had taken their degrees at Columbia, five at Johns Hopkins. By 1900, Hopkins had turned out at least 30 Ph.D.'s who would shortly become members of the Association; Columbia had been almost half as productive.[29]

Political science as taught at Johns Hopkins was not identical to the subject as taught at Columbia, but the intellectual bases had much in common. Both were "specifically designed to train professional scholars"; both were based on European, mainly German, models; both were heavily research oriented; both employed the seminar.[30] But there were also several differences: at Columbia coursework and theses covered a wide range of subject matter and the faculty stressed comparative analysis and collection of statistical data; at Hopkins the subjects were generally confined to American institutional and economic history, with stress on the historical approach.[31]

By the turn of the twentieth century, political science, as an academic discipline, was well established in American universities. In most cases, the programs were copied from the Columbia or Hopkins program or were attempts to create a hybrid of the two. Columbia and Johns Hopkins so thoroughly dominated the field that there was virtually no other model available. Graduates of those two programs became the teachers at other colleges and universities, including such institutions as Chicago, Illinois,

Indiana, Michigan, Minnesota, Missouri, Pennsylvania, Princeton, and Texas. These were primarily undergraduate teaching assignments, although other graduate departments were organized even before the turn of the century. Those included programs at Michigan (1881-1887) under Dean Charles K. Adams; Pennsylvania (1885-1889) under Edmund J. James; and at Brown, Wisconsin, and Chicago.

Harvard did not yet have a graduate program in government, but A. Lawrence Lowell was elected in 1900 to the newly created chair of the "Science of Government." The chair was endowed by Cyrus Eaton, who insisted on naming the position with the term used by George Washington. The title of the chair pleased Lowell, who advocated the application of scientific methods to government; and Lowell's introductory course, Government I, became so popular that a new lecture hall had to be built (with funds contributed anonymously by Lowell himself) to house it.[32]

Having become an accepted part of the professional academic establishment, political science inevitably became organized. Graduate departments had been founded and the *Political Science Quarterly* was regularly publishing the results of the research and deliberations of academic political scientists. As with history and economics, so with political science, the founding of a national association was the next step. One historian of the American university has summarized this tendency as follows: "The graduate school fostered a high degree of professionalism in intellectual life. Organizations of those engaged in the various academic specialties spread from the natural sciences to other disciplines."[33]

On the morning of 28 December 1904, Professor Frank J. Goodnow, president of the American Political Science Association, called to order the first full-scale public meeting of that organization. The meeting climaxed two years of preparatory work. A gathering of "leading practitioners" of political science had been held at Washington, D.C., on 30 December 1902 to consider founding an "American Society for Comparative Legislation." Those who attended decided that the proposed society was too narrow in scope, and they selected a committee, headed by Professor Jeremiah Jencks of Cornell, to consider founding a society with the entire field of political science as its domain. A meeting called by Jencks's committee was held at New Orleans in December 1903 in conjunction with a joint meeting of the American Historical Association and the American Economics Association and on 30 December 1903 the twenty-five people who attended the meeting voted the American Political Science Association into existence. The consequences of that decision for the academicization and professionalization of the discipline are the subject of a later part of the instant work.

The rapid acceptance of political science as a separate and legitimate discipline, and the common experience of most of the active members of the profession, gave to the membership of the fledgling association a remarkable homogeneity of viewpoint about what their discipline ought to be and how it ought to proceed. It is the content and significance of that viewpoint that this study is meant to explore. While it is no doubt true that the first American political scientists were the products of their times, it is true as well that they were shapers of their times. Unlike most contemporary political scientists, most members of the founding generation did not regard practical politics as "extrascientific activity"[34] but as the source of direction for their scientific activity and the field upon which that activity was ultimately played out.

That attitude was one product of the "revolt" within the discipline against its first parents. The revolt occurred so early and was so thorough that it must be regarded as part of the founding process itself; and it is the reason why Burgess's influence over the discipline, although great, was primarily as a "negative reference."[35] "By the late 1880s," as Michael Frisch has reported, "the first generation to come through American graduate training was already turning the comparative method against the idealism of Burgess and Adams."[36] Burgess and Adams had taught their students, in part, to look to local institutions to find the character of the nation. When the students looked at American local institutions, and especially at urban institutions, what they saw was corruption, boss rule, and inefficiency. A large number of these students turned their attention to developing the methods for reform. "Nothing was more central to this revolt than the emerging study of public law and administration."[37]

The association founded in 1903-1904 reflected those interests. Most of the members who were academics were also members of the American Historical Association or the American Economic Association, or both, and a good number of the founding members were faculty members or graduates of either Columbia or Johns Hopkins where public law and administration were emphasized. The first president of the new association, Frank J. Goodnow, was Burgess's own choice to teach public administration at Columbia.

But Goodnow, and most of the active members of the new group, stood well to the left of Burgess. The American Political Science Association had a political program—implementation of progressive social reform measures. The "science" of which they were the official spokesmen was not neutral in that regard. The first four presidents of the A.P.S.A. (Goodnow, Bryce, Lowell, and Wilson) "had a strong belief in common that political studies must have direct relevance to practical politics."[38] The understanding of the association's founders has been characterized as the belief "that a systematic understanding of politics (as a necessary prelude to reform) had been bedeviled by excessive discussion of how [it] should work."[39] Bernard Crick has described the dominant position of the founding leaders of the APSA as follows:

> A firm separation was demanded between normative and factual propositions. "Ends" were broadly apolitical question for popular electoral decision; "means" towards those ends, and the knowledge that would contribute towards making these means efficient-these could be a much-more-than-less scientific question.[40]

The Association's official journal, the *American Political Science Review* began publication in November 1906. One effect of publication of the *Review* was that a certain homogeneity of opinion about the methods, purposes, and conclusions of political science was thereby assured. "The official understanding of what was 'sound' political science could be ignored only by the most illustrious or the most foolhardy and stubborn practitioners. In this sense, the *Review* molded no less than it mirrored.[41]

For writers about the history of academic political science, the founding of the Association has sometimes appeared as a watershed. For example, Bernard Crick describes a "break between the post-Civil War generation of political science and the pragmatists of the 1900."[42] To be sure, there were changes at about that time. Herbert B. Adams died in 1901. John W. Burgess, although he continued to publish the *Political Science Quarterly*, retired from active teaching and professional involvement about the same time. In fact, however, there was a great deal of continuity of thought right up to the beginning of the First World War.

The greatest change that occurred after the turn of the century was the remarkably fast growth of the profession. There are various ways to measure that growth; for example, membership in the American Political Science Association increased from 214 in 1904 to 1350 in 1910 and to 1462 in 1915.[43] Another indication of growth is the fact that thirty-eight colleges and universities had established separate departments of political science by 1914.[44] Still another measure of growth is annual Ph.D. production in American graduate schools: 1885–1900, 34; 1900–1910, 610; 1911–1915, 1015.[45]

Columbia and Johns Hopkins continued to produce the bulk of new doctorates. Columbia granted approximately twenty Ph.D. degrees from 1901 to 1910 and about forty between 1911 and 1920. Johns Hopkins awarded six Ph.D. degrees from 1901 to 1910 and eighteen between 1911 and 1920. Wisconsin, Harvard, Pennsylvania, and Chicago also awarded the doctorate in political science, but "their combined production did not vastly exceed Columbia's alone."[46]

The founding of the A.P.S.A. began a decade of development characterized by the redirection of the discipline toward public administration. That, in turn, was a product of the "revolt" of the first American Ph.D.s against the German-trained founders of their graduate schools. The revolt at Columbia was led by Frank J. Goodnow, but there were "parallel developments at Johns Hopkins, where the young Woodrow Wilson was forging an original and widely-noted critique of American politics with administrative theory at its center."[47]

The theme of this whole study is the replacement of the traditional American political science by a new science of politics located in the university and dominated by professors who were also professionals. The "revolt," as Frisch calls it, was but a variation on that theme. The young critics of the founders of the new political science did not seek to counterattack on behalf of the earlier tradition; rather they meant to carry on the reform and redirection that their teachers had begun. It was not that the founders had gone in the wrong direction, on the contrary, but that, in the opinion of their students and protégés, they had not gone far enough in the direction they had chosen.

The high point and low point of academic political science came within two years of each other early in the second decade of the twentieth century. In 1912, Woodrow Wilson, a Johns Hopkins Ph.D., a professor of political science, author of widely read works on politics and public administration, and third president of the American Political Science Association, himself was elected president of the United States. Surely the time had come when the fruits of professional political science would be put to use in the national government.

Then, in 1914, the two most progressive nations in the world, the nations from whom American political scientists had learned what they knew about politics and administration, the nations whose political success proved that history could be relied upon to yield ever more progress in public affairs, Britain and Germany, went to war. And this was perhaps the darkest hour for American political science. Willoughby wrote *Prussian Political Philosophy*, showing that the *allgeneine*

Staatslehre of Bluntschli and Treitschke led to Germany's aggressive impulses. Burgess, whose quest for a new science of politics had begun on the battlefield of the American Civil War wrote in despair that the quest had been in vain, for the new political science had not averted this much greater civil war.

After World War I, there was a more serious revolt within the discipline, led by Charles Merriam and beginning with the publication of his *New Aspects in Politics* in 1921. That, too, was a revolt, and not a revolution, although historians concerned primarily with methodology would identify it as the real watershed. At least until that point, if not since then, the history of American political science is a continuous story. Even Somit and Tannenhaus concede that neither 1903 nor any other date from 1880 to 1921 marked dramatic changes in thinking about the nature of political science or about the responsibilities of its practitioners.[48]

Throughout the whole period, political science was dominated by an ideology of progress. Human society was envisaged as capable of permanent and perpetual improvement, and the state was the chosen instrument for accomplishing that improvement. That ideology was never challenged within the discipline, and, in fact, continues to dominate the discipline even into its second century.

NOTES

1. Frank J. Goodnow, *Social Reform and the Constitution* (New York: The Macmillan Company, 1911), 1.

2. Albert Somit and Joseph Tannenhaus, Development, *The Development of American Political Science: From Burgess to Behavioralism* (Boston: Allyn and Bacon, Inc., 1967), 2.

3. Bernard Crick, American Science, *The American Science of Politics: Its Origins and Conditions* (Berkeley: University of California Press, 1959), 69.

4. Crick, American Science, *American Science*, 69.

5. Richard Hofstadter, "The Development of Higher Education in America," in Hofstadter and C. DeWitt Hardy, *The Development and Scope of Higher Education in the United States* (New York: Columbia University Press, 1952), 29–30.

6. Laurence R. Veysey, *The Emergence of the American University* (Chicago: University of Chicago Press, 1965), 1, quoting G. Stanley Hall's Phi Beta Kappa oration of 1891.

7. Somit and Tannenhaus, Development, *Development*, 22.

8. Veysey, *Emergence*, 2–3.

9. Anna Haddow, *The Study of Political Science in American Colleges and Universities: 1636–1900* (New York: D. Appleton Century Company, 1939), 171–221 and *passim*.

10. John D. Millett, "The Department of Public Law and Government" in R. Gordon Hoxie, et al., *A History of the Faculty of Political Science, Columbia University* (Morningside Heights, N.Y.: Columbia University Press, 1955), 256–257; Crick, *American Science*, 16; Haddow, *Study of Political Science*, 122–123.

11. John W. Burgess, *Reminiscences of an American Scholar: The Beginnings of Columbia University* (Morningside Heights, N.Y.: Columbia University Press, 1934), 194–195; Haddow, *Study of Political Science*, 178–182.

12. Crick, *American Science*, 106.

13. Somit and Tannenhaus, *Development*, 52.

14. Crick, *American Science*, 97.

15. Crick, *American Science*, 97.

16. Somit and Tannenhaus, *Development*, 3.

17. Michael H. Frisch, "Urban Theorists," "Urban Theorists, Urban Reform, and American Political Culture in the Progressive Period," *Political Science Quarterly* 97, no. 2 (Summer 1982): 299.

18. Burgess, *Reminiscences*, 29.

19. Burgess, *Reminiscences*, 69.

20. Burgess, *Reminiscences*, 70–71; Edward B. Brown, *American Conservatives: The Political Thought of Francis Lieber and John W. Burgess* (New York: Columbia University Press, 1951), p. ca. 80.

21. Burgess, *Reminiscences*, 71.

22. Burgess, *Reminiscences*, 50.

23. Burgess, *Reminiscences*, 85.

24. Millett, "Department," 257.

25. Burgess, *Reminiscences*, 194–195; Hofstadter, "Development," 62–63.

26. Somit and Tannenhaus, *Development*, 21.

27. Hofstadter, "Development," 63.

28. This motto, painted on the wall in large letters, can be clearly seen in a photograph of the seminar room included in Henry W. Bragdon, *Woodrow Wilson: The Academic Years* (Cambridge, Mass.: Belknap Press of Harvard University Press, 1967), following 20.

29. Somit and Tannenhaus, *Development*, 34–35.

30. Somit and Tannenhaus, *Development*, 34–35.

31. Somit and Tannenhaus, *Development*, 36–37.

32. Crick, *American Science*, 104–105.

33. Hofstadter, "Development," 64.

34. Somit and Tannenhaus, *Development*, 42–48, 80–85.

35. Frisch, "Urban Theorists," 299.

36. Frisch, "Urban Theorists," 300.

37. Frisch, "Urban Theorists," 300–301.

38. Crick, *American Science*, 101.

39. Crick, *American Science*, 101.

40. Crick, *American Science*, 101.

41. Somit and Tannenhaus, *Development*, 54.

42. Crick, *American Science*, 99.

43. Somit and Tannenhaus, *Development*, 55.

44. Somit and Tannenhaus, *Development*, 56.

45. Somit and Tannenhaus, *Development*, 58, their estimates.

46. Somit and Tannenhaus, *Development*, 58–59, is the source for all figures.

47. Frisch, "Urban Theorists," 301.

48. Somit and Tannenhaus, *Development*, 63.

Part I

ORIGINS AND INFLUENCES

Chapter One

GERMAN POLITICAL SCIENCE

The principal influence on American political science during the period of its emergence as an independent academic discipline was the science of politics as taught and practiced in the German universities. The creation of the American discipline was a part of what Perry Miller has called "one of the most radical revolutions in the history of the American mind," the invasion of the American university by German idealism.[1] The intellectual historian Juergen Herbst, chronicling that invasion, aptly characterized it as "a transfer of culture."[2]

German political science—*Staatswissenschaft*—was not merely an academic discipline, but a practical science of political organization: *episteme politike* in the classical sense. The professors in the universities were also the counselers and advisers of the government; indeed, many of them were legislators or bureaucrats as well as professors. The efficacy of their political science was demonstrated in their lifetime by the unification of Germany under Prussian hegemony and the creation of the German Empire.

The university professors, and especially the professors of history and law were at the core of what historian Fritz Ringer has called the German "mandarin" class. Ringer defined the "mandarins" simply as a social and cultural elite which owes its status primarily to educational qualifications, rather than to hereditary rights or wealth. The "mandarin

intellectuals," chiefly the university professors, are concerned with the
intellectual diet of the elite. They uphold the standards of qualification
for membership in the group and they act as its spokesman in cultural
questions.[3]

The elite thus defined came, in the Germany of 1870 to 1890 "to
supply an ever growing portion of the state officials" within a state
apparatus run "according to fixed and logical principles and which
[stood] above both rulers and ruled."[4] German political science was
therefore eminently practical, it was the political science of the administrators of the German state.

The influence of this German political science upon its fledgling
American counterpart is to be seen in several ways: first, in the lives of
the American founding generation; second, in the citations and references in their professional work; third, and most important, in the
concerns, the methods, and the assumptions of American political
science as evidenced in the books, articles, and lectures of the founding
generation.

Biographically, the evidence is unambiguous. In the formative years
of the founding fathers of the new discipline (a period of roughly two
decades following the end of the Civil War) there was no real graduate
school in the United States; certainly there was no graduate department
of political science. Aspiring scholars were forced to go abroad if they
desired to continue their studies beyond the bachelor level. It was
Germany that had the strongest attraction for them. This was especially
so for students of politcs and public law, who were unable to find their
chosen course of study in any American college or university. Germany
was the site of a flourishing academic life, and the home of the new
political science, and so drew the young scholars to herself. The elderly
historian, George Bancroft, was American ambassador at Berlin, and
personally directed the studies of a chosen few.

The German university occupied a place in the cultural and political
life of the German states, and later of the German empire, unlike that
occupied by American colleges or even other European universities. In a
lecture given at the end of the period treated in the present study, John
Dewey reported:

> Germany is the modern state which provides the greatest facilities for
> general ideas to take effect through social inculcation. Its system of
> ideas is adapted to that end. Higher schools and universities are really,
> not just nominally, under the control of the state and part of the state
> life. . . . Moreover, one of the chief functions of the universities is the

preparation of future state officers. Legislative activity is distinctly subordinate to that of administration conducted by a trained civil service, or, if you please, bureaucracy. Membership in this bureaucracy is dependent upon university training.[5]

The American students who sought out this experience not only sat at the feet of the intellectual leaders of the German nation but also sat among the young men who would shortly be carrying on the daily business of the German empire.

Even this does not fully describe the position of the university in the German political order. Dewey ascribed to it the function of creating and molding public opinion:

> Public opinion hardly exists in Germany in the sense in which it obtains in France, Great Britain, or this country. So far as it exists, the universities may be said to be its chief organs. They, rather than the newspapers, crystallize it and give it articulate expression.[6]

Of course, educational institutions always participate in the formation of public opinion, but this was true in a special sense in that regime where the opinion that counted was that of the "mandarin" class.

There can be no doubt that the practical success, or apparent success, of the German *Staatswissenschaft* was a large part of the attraction. John W. Burgess, for example, related in his memoirs how he found his vocation as a political scientist while serving as a Southerner in the Union Army. There must be a science of politics, he imagined, that could prevent civil war and insure peace, first within a nation and then among nations.[7] He recorded his search for such a science in American academia and law, and finally his discovery of that science in Germany.[8] His certainty that he had found the object of his quest was dated from his observation of the procession of the returned emperor and his troops following their victory in the Franco-Prussian War.[9]

In just two years in Germany, under the guidance of Ambassador Bancroft, Burgess enrolled successively at three German universities, Goettingen, Leipzig, and Berlin. He attended the lectures of the most distinguished professors of history and public law, including Ernst Curtius, Theodore Mommsen, and Rudolf H. Lotze. But the most lasting impression was made on him by his tutor, Gustav Droysen (the official historiographer of the Prussian state and director of research in the state archives)[10], and Heinrich von Treitschke (whose summer courses Burgess returned in subsequent years to attend)[11] and, especially,

Rudolph von Gneist. The latter was Bismarck's legal adviser and "the teacher . . . who led me in the line of the work to which my subsequent professional life was chiefly devoted."[12]

Burgess, of course, was the founder of the School of Political Science at Columbia University and head of the first graduate department of politics in the United States. He sent his first handful of graduate student-disciples to Germany to retrace his pilgrimage, so that the whole of the original faculty of political science at Columbia University spent at least a year studying in German universities. That original faculty included Richmond Mayo-Smith (Berlin, Paris), Edmund M. Smith (Berlin), and Clifford R. Bateman (Heidelberg).

The School of Political Science was founded in conscious imitation of the seminar system used in the German universities[13] and in the Ecole Libre des Sciences Politiques at Paris. As a concession to the common student, however, the Columbia program provided closer supervision and more frequent examinations. "We felt that the European system produced a splendid aristocracy of scholars, but also we felt it our duty to do something for democracy, even in letters and science."[14]

In addition, historian Herbert Baxter Adams and economist Richard T. Ely, whose joint seminar at Johns Hopkins University (whence were graduated both Woodrow Wilson and Westel W. Willoughby) was the second spawning ground of American political science, both received their graduate training in Germany. The founders of Johns Hopkins invited Andrew D. White, of Cornell, to address them on the subject of "education in political science" in 1879. He, too, advocated the German model:

> What is now proposed is no longer a new thing. In Germany, for many years, extended courses of instruction in history, politics and social science and general jurisprudence have been presented in various universities and have had great influence for good; it is undoubtedly true that the want of practical political instruction, —that instruction which comes by taking part directly in political affairs, has prevented complete and well-founded political development in Germany; but to the influence of these courses is due, in an immense degree, that excellence in German administration which is at last acknowledged and admired by the entire world.[15]

The "*Herren Doktoren*," the Americans trained in German universities, and their students were the first professors of political science in the new American universities, just then being constructed on the German model. Political science was not unique in this; as Herbst has pointed out, in all the disciplines "the returning scholars made possible the rapid growth of American graduate education in the 1880s and 1890s" and "introduced German ideals into undergraduate as well as graduate education."[16]

The influence is acknowledged as well in the written work of the first American political scientists. To examine the footnotes and bibliographies of the early published works is to encounter the names and titles of German academics and their books: Bluntschli, Treitschke, Jellinek, Gneist, Stengel, Kirchenhem, Sarwey, Meyer, Loening, Droysen, Curtius, Mommsen, and so on. Moreover, of the books reviewed in the *Political Science Quarterly* from its founding to the turn of the twentieth century, more than a sixth (an average of twenty titles per year) were written in German.

The German political science was the model for the new American political science. It was desirable of imitation because of the level of scientific sophistication it had achieved, and also because of its practical successes. But the German political science was more than a model—it was also a starting point. The assumptions and methods which had served the German school were adopted, by and large, by the American founding generation. Of course, the German school was problematic for Americans. Its idealism was unabashedly aristocratic, while that of the Americans, at least after Burgess, was wholly democratic. But the terms of discourse were adopted almost without question.

What was this German political science? In a general sense, it was the *Staatswissenschaft*. That is, the field of study that has the State as its object. As Ringer has written:

> In German usage, any organized body of information is referred to as *eine Wissenschaft* . . . At the same time, all formal knowledge, and the collective activity of scholars in obtaining, interpreting, and ordering it, may be rendered . . . *die Wissenschaft*. I.e., *Wissenschaft* simply means a discipline." [17]

But the discipline called *Staatswissenschaft* was dominated, in the second half of the nineteenth century, by *allgemeine Staatslehere*, or "general State theory." At the most basic, it is Hegel's historical dialectic; its emphasis is always collective, rather than individualistic. It was founded by Dahlmann and Bluntschli and given final expression by Treitschke. It was distinguished by its object, the State; by its method, historical-comparative; and by its goal, perfection of the State apparatus.

The term "State" (*Staat*) does not correspond to the English word "state," still less to either "government" or "nation." The State was described as the organic expression of the national character and national will, through the constitution, the unwritten laws and customs, statutory enactments, kings and parliaments, and the body politic. The State so understood embraced the living citizens, but it was not the same as the citizens and it was not theirs to alter.

Properly, there should be one State for each nation. The formula used by the two postwar German republics when they recognized each other ("two German States within one German nation") would have been unintelligible to the practitioners of the German political science (and was, probably for that very reason, acceptable to both German governments). The State, like any organic being, evolves, or grows, over time. Because some nations are more progressive than others, States exist at the same time in different evolutionary stages.

The State is neither wholly by nature nor wholly conventional. It exists in history, that is to say, in its own evolution. The study of politics, then, begins with the study of history. But history is unidirectional. Since the State is not susceptible of being understood by rational principles apart from the history of its own evolution, there is neither better nor worse about it, but only more advanced and less advanced, newer and older. The State evolves through stages, and all States seem to evolve through the same stages. Therefore, by comparison of one State with another, it is possible to see which are the advanced (progressive) States, and which the backward. The political scientist can hasten the evolution of individual States by transferring the technology of the State from the more advanced to the less advanced. Hence the desirability of comparative political studies.

The originator of this Hegelian science of politics was Friedrich C. Dahlmann (1785–1860). Dahlmann sought to put political science on a historical basis, but he did not produce any systematic work along those lines. Like his disciples and successors, Dahlmann was active in politics, and regarded his political activity as an appropriate complement to his academic work.

The British historian Lewis Namier, writing in the 1950s, referred to Dahlmann as "probably the most eminent intellectual in the Frankfurt Parliament" that attempted in 1848–1849 to establish a federal German empire with a constitutional monarch at the head.[18] Dahlmann prepared the first draft of the imperial constitution promulgated by the Frankfurt

Parliament, and did so in one week, saying that he hoped "with a few incisive paragraphs to heal the ills of a thousand years."[19]

Johann K. Bluntschli (1808–1881), though a Swiss, was trained in Germany and taught in Germany. He was associated most closely with the University of Freiburg-im-Breisgau in Baden. In politics, he was an intense pan-German nationalist, and favored the unification of the German states under Prussia. Bluntschli's political science was based upon a general theory of the State (*allgemeine Staatslehre*) which equated the body politic to a living organism. Bluntschli's influence on Westel W. Willoughby is most evident in a comparison of Bluntschli's book entitled *Allgemeine Staatslehre* with Willoughby's *The Nature of the State*.

The most influential member of the German school was Heinrich von Treitschke (1834–1896). A pupil of Dahlmann's and a onetime colleague of Bluntschli's at Freiburg, he taught, from 1874 on, at the University of Berlin. A fervent advocate of German unification under Prussian hegemony, he served in the Reichstag and was the official historian of the Prussian state as well as a professor. Treitschke's *allgemeine Staatslehre* was more rigorous and systematic than Bluntschlils, though no less organic or historicist.

Others of the same general school included Theodore Mommsen and Rudolph von Gneist. These are names well known to students of history, for (as follows rather clearly from the notion that the State is the working out of the Absolute in history and that political knowledge knowledge of that historical process) the German science of politics was not to be distinguished from the study of history.

Treitschke described political science as having three ends:

> The task of political science is a threefold one. In the first place, it must endeavour, from a consideration of actually existing states, to discover the fundamental conceptions underlying the State. It must then examine historically the political aims, activities, and achievements of the various nations, as well as the reason why they have achieved what they have achieved; and in the course of this it will accomplish the third part of its task, namely, the discovery; of certain historical laws and the establishment of certain moral imperatives. Considered in this way, political science is applied history.[20]

Treitscke's "applied history" would lead to "the proper systematic study of political science, such as was perhaps contemplated by Bluntschli."[21]

Treitschke's political science was *Staatswissenschaft*—the science of the State—and was founded upon *Staatslehre*—the theory of the State. The State, and not the individual, was the object of the science because Treitschke regarded the State "as a being which is infinitely superior to the individual, which exists to realise an ideal beyond and above that of individual happiness."[22] Treitschke defined the State as "a People (*Volk*) united by legal ties to form an independent power,"[23] and, like Bluntschli, Treitschke was "prepared to think of the State as a person in the moral as well as in the legal sense."[24]

This concept of the State was attributable to the Hegelian school, if not to Hegel himself. John Dewey summarized the German academic teaching concerning the State as follows:

> [T]he State, if not avowedly something mystic and transcendental, is at least a moral entity, the creation of a self-conscious reason operating in behalf of the spiritual and ideal interests of its members. Its function is cultural, educative. . . . [I]t is the duty of the State to intervene so that the struggle [for honor and status] may contribute to ideal ends . . . Unlike other forms of force, it has a sort of sacred import, for it represents force consecrated to the assertion and expansion of final goods which are spiritual, moral, rational.[25]

Moreover, the State has a special place in history:

> The State is the Individual of history; it is to history what a given man is to biography. History gives us the progressive realization or evolution of the Absolute, moving from one National Individual to another. It is the law, the universal, which makes the State a State, for the law is reason. . . . [W]hen citizens of a state (especially of the state in which this philosophic insight has been achieved) take the laws of their state as their own ends and motives of action, they attain the best possible substitute for a reason which is its own object.[26]

It is in this sense that the concept of the State was imported from German political science into American political science.

The earliest writings of the new founders of the new American political science carried these assumptions over virtually intact. The object of the American science of politics was to be "the State," and the definition and discussion in the works of Willoughby,[27] Goodnow,[28] and especially Burgess,[29] correspond to the discussion in those of Bluntschli and Treitschke. Woodrow Wilson, in his tome on *The State*, never offers a definition of his subject but he seems, throughout, to assume the terms of the German discussion.

Even the racism was carried over, especially in Wilson and Burgess. Burgess, for example, calls the "Teutonic nations" the "Political nations, par excellence," and calls the national state "the peculiar creation of these nations."[30] Because the national state is "the most modern and the most complete solution of the whole problem of political organization," the political genius of the Teutonic nations that created it entitle them "to assume the leadership in the establishment and administration of states."[31] Wilson confined his discourse to the history of those European and American governments which have constituted the order of social life for those stronger and nobler races which have made the most notable progress in civilization.[32]

Burgess, of course, introduced this German-style political science to his students at Columbia and to others through his books. To the student of Burgess

> [t]he influence of Hegel, to whom Burgess had been introduced by Droysen and Treitschke, and had been prepared by Seelye, is undeniable. . . . It is clear that Burgess was chiefly indebted to Hegel for his concept of historical process. In addition, he apparently was following Bluntschli in distinguishing history from political science and political science from constitutional (or public) law.[33]

Burgess defined the State as "a particular portion of mankind viewed as an organized unit"; then, in a footnote, quoted Bluntschli's definition: "The State is the politically organized national person [*Volksperson*] of a definite country."[34] Although Burgess's own words are susceptible of interpretation according to what John Dewey said was the standard Anglo-American understanding ("[i]n English and American writings, the State is almost always used to denote society in its more organized aspects"[35]), the quotation from Bluntschli reveals what Burgess has in mind. Burgess went on to identify four characteristics of the State: comprehensiveness, exclusivity, permanence, and sovereignty.[36] By "sovereignty," Burgess meant "original, absolute, unlimited, universal power over the individual subject and over all associations of subjects."[37]

The next generation of American political scientists did not adhere so rigidly to the German categories used by Burgess. But the disagreement with Burgess was within the larger analytical framework he had created, and reached only certain particulars of Burgess's teaching. For example, as intellectual historian Bernard Brown wrote:

Willoughby rejected Burgess's particular distinction between state and government. Sovereignty, he held, is the exclusive power of the State to determine its own attributes and rights. It is indivisible, and must rest in the lawmaking organs. Similarly, Woodrow Wilson distinguished the power of government (sovereignty) from the right of the community to control that government.[38]

Brown, as a historian of American political thought, attributed this disagreement to the difference in political program between Burgess and the younger men. "Burgess' theory of sovereignty," Brown wrote, "had to be modified by those who felt the necessity for increased government regulation of private property relations."[39] Burgess, who thought it possible to distinguish a sphere of government from a sphere of liberty, did not want to admit a fundamental unity of State and government. What he did not realize was that the political science he taught could not sustain such a distinction. Burgess's political theory of race is traceable directly to roots in German political science:

> Bluntschli suggested that different races have different capacities and endowments; Heinrich Treitschke urged the necessity of imperialism for civilized nations, and related the poltical capacity of races to claims for independent statehood; while Hegel thought that each national grouping had a "mission" to fulfill.[40]

Burgess divided European peoples into three groups, Teutonic, Romanic, and Slavonic. And, although Brown claimed that Burgess "tended to discount racial differences in the development of the national state, he glorified race as a factor in the evaluation of individuals and nations."[41] The Teutonic peoples included the Germans and the British, and, unless the nation were polluted by the immigration of less progressive types, the Americans. To these peoples belonged the "mission to establish states upon the principle of national union and independence, and to take the leadership in the administration of these states."[42] The Teutons alone, Burgess thought, were capable of political action.

A salient theme in the literature of the new political science was that of collectivism, or of treating the State as the primary phenomenon and the individual as secondary. This reflected the influence of the German historical school. As Juergen Herbst wrote:

To view and evaluate man as a member of a group rather than as an individual invited reliance on a nonindividualistic philosophy such as was offered by the Hegelians. Once the post-Civil War migration to German universities had begun, the results were soon evident. . . . In the hands of such teachers as [Ely and Burgess] the Hegelian dialectic explained and superseded individualistic moral philosophy, ushering in a more socially minded instruction in ethics, which was advanced by the new disciplines of social science.[43]

Burgess, although he personally favored a more restricted sphere of governmental power, refused to treat liberty as something to which individuals had a right. Following Hegel, he argued that "no constitution should undertake to except anything from the power of the state as organized in the Constitution."

Nevertheless, the most important theme to be carried over from the German science of politics into the new American science of politics was the doctrine of inevitable progress toward the nation state. Summarizing the teaching of Treitschke, Burgess wrote: "He held always most tenaciously to the track of historic evolution."[44] A sweeping statement of the doctrine of progress, wholly compatible with the theories of the German historical school, is found in Wilson's treatise on the State:

From the dim morning hours of history when the father was king and priest down to this modern time of history's high noon when nations stand forth full grown and self-governed, the law of coherence and continuity in political development has suffered no serious breach. . . . Tested by history's long measurements, the lines of advance are seen to be singularly straight.[45]

But, in this, Wilson was hardly less sweeping than Burgess:

The proposition that the state is the product of history means that it is the gradual and continuous development of human society, out of a grossly imperfect beginning, through crude but improving forms of manifestation, towards a perfect and universal organization of mankind.[46]

James W. Garner, in his introductory treatise, quoted this passage from Burgess as "high authority," and found himself "led to the conclusion that the state . . . is an institution of natural growth, of historical evolution."[47] He went on to write that "aided by the forces of history . . .

uncivilized peoples are brought out of anarchy and subjected to the authority of the state."[48] Raymond G. Gettel, writing at the same time, asserted:

> This progress has taken different forms and has proceeded with varying rapidity among different peoples. . . . [L]aw and authority have taken on a human rather than a supernatural sanction; and the need for order and protection, due to the increasing complexity of economic and social life has become the chief reason for political life. . . . [A]nd the state, no longer looked upon with dread as a tyrannous monster, has entered upon a constantly widening sphere of usefulness.[49]

In a later work Gettell averred that only in recent times has "the fixity of primitive ideas been replaced by the ideal of progress, and . . . the modern state has developed."[50]

To the German influence also may be ascribed the primacy of administration in the work of American political science. In his lecture at Johns Hopkins on "education in political science," Andrew D. White praised the German educational system for perfecting public administration and said: "We may disbelieve in the general theories of government prevalent among the Germans, but we cannot deny the excellence of their administration."[51] Similarly, Woodrow Wilson, who took his Ph.D. degree from Johns Hopkins seven years after White's lecture, wrote that public administration was "a foreign science . . . developed by French and German professors."[52]

American political science began in conscious imitation of the German *Staatswissenschaft* and *Staatslehre*. Even so, as Brown wrote, it took on distinctly American characteristics. "While the political thought of both Lieber and Burgess was clearly German in origin, it must be remembered that their theories were articulated under American conditions."[53] Eventually the direct influence of German academic political science was attenuated by two other main influences, the political reform impulse of the Progressive movement and the intellectual movement called pragmatism (each of which was, in turn, influenced by Hegelianism) to give American political science its unique character.

NOTES

1.   Perry Miller, *American Thought: Civil War to World War I* (New York: Rinehart & Co., Inc., 1954), ix.

2. Jurgen Herbst, *The German Historical School in American Scholarship: A Study in the Transfer of Culture* (Ithaca, N.Y.: Cornell University Press, 1965).

3. Fritz K. Ringer, Decline, *The Decline of the German Mandarins: The German Academic Community, 1890–1933* (Cambridge, Mass.: Harvard University Press, 1969), 6.

4. Ringer, *Decline*, 9.

5. John Dewey, *German Philosophy and Politics* (Freeport, N.Y.: Books for Libraries Press, 1970), 59–60. [Originally published in 1915; new introductory material added in 1945.]

6. Dewey, *German Philosophy*, 61.

7. John W. Burgess, *Reminiscences of an American Scholar* (Boston: Houghton-Mifflin Company, 1931), 69–71, 86.

8. Burgess, *Reminiscences*, 69, 84–84, 99–131.

9. Burgess, *Reminiscences*, 96.

10. Burgess, *Reminiscences*, 126–127.

11. Burgess, *Reminiscences*, 129–130.

12. Burgess, *Reminiscences*, 131.

13. Burgess, *Reminiscences*, 190, 197–200.

14. Burgess, *Reminiscences*, 199.

15. Andrew D. White, *Education in Political Science* (Baltimore: Johns Hopkins University Press, 1880), 21.

16. Herbst, *German Historical*, 24.

17. Ringer, *Decline*, 102–103.

18. Lewis Namier, "History" reprinted in *The Varieties of History: From Voltaire to the Present* ed by Fritz Stern (New York: Meridian Books, 1956), 375. [This essay was originally published in Namier's *Avenues of History*, 1952.]

19. Namier, "History," 375.

20. Heinrich von Treitschke, *Politik*, translated by Winifred Ray for H. W. C. Davis, Political Thought, *The Political Thought of Heinrich von Treitschke* (New York: Charles Scribner's Sons, 1915), 121.

21. Treitschke, *Politik*, 122.

22. Davis, *Political Thought*, 120.

23. Davis, *Political Thought*, 127.

24. Davis, *Political Thought*, 129.

25. Dewey, *German Philosophy*, 96.

26. Dewey, *German Philosophy*, 132–133.

27. Westel W. Willoughby, *An Examination of the Nature of the State: A Study in Political Philosophy* (New York: Macmillan and Co., 1896), 8–9.

28. Frank J. Goodnow, *Politics and Administration: A Study in Government* (New York: Russell & Russell, 1967), 1–22.

29. John W. Burgess, *Political Science and Comparative Constitutional Law* (Boston: Ginn & Company, 1890), vol. I, 49–58.

30. Burgess, *Political Science*, vol. I, 37.

31. Burgess, *Political Science*, vol. I, 39.

32. Woodrow Wilson, *The State: Elements of Historical and Practical Politics* (Boston: D.C. Heath & Co., Publishers, 1897), 2.

33. Bernard Edward Brown, *American Conservatives: The Political Thought of Francis Lieber and John W. Burgess* (New York: Columbia University Press, 1951), 118–119.

34. Burgess, *Political Science*, vol. I, 50. The footnote is in German, and it quotes from Bluntschli's *Theory of the Modern State*, vol. I, 24; the passage is found in the "authorized translation" at 23.

35. Dewey, *German Philosophy*, 95.

36. Burgess, *Political Science*, vol. I, 52–53.

37. Burgess, *Political Science*, vol. I, 52–53.

38. Brown, *American Conservatives*, 150.

39. Brown, *American Conservatives*, 130.

40. Brown, *American Conservatives*, 134.

41. Brown, *American Conservatives*, 131.

42. Brown, *American Conservatives*, 133.

43. Herbst, *German Historical*, 67.

44. Burgess, *Reminiscences*, 130.

45. Wilson, *The State*, 575–576.

46. Burgess, *Political Science*, vol. I, 59.

47. James W. Garner, *Introduction to Political Science* (New York: American Book Company, 1910), 120.

48. Garner, *Introduction*, 122.

49. Raymond G. Gettell, *Introduction to Political Science* (Boston: Ginn and Company, 1910), 50–51.

50. Raymond G. Gettell, *Problems in Political Evolution* (Boston: Ginn and Company, 1914), 101.

51. White, *Education in Political Science*, 21.

52. Woodrow Wilson, "The Study of Administration," in *College and State: Educational, Literary and Political Papers (1875–1913)*, ed. by R. S. Baker and W. E. Dodd (New York: Harper & Brothers, Publishers, 1925), vol. I, 131.

53. Brown, *American Conservatives*, 173.

Chapter Two

PRAGMATISM

The second major influence on American political science in its early days was the school of thought called "pragmatism." Frank J. Goodnow, noting that "[m]ore and more political and social students are recognizing that a policy of opportunism is the policy most likely to be followed by desirable results," equated that "feeling" to the teachings of the "pragmatic school" in philosophy.[1] Goodnow acknowledged the influence of pragmatism on his own and his contemporaries' political science without professing to subscribe to its dogmas:

> One may, therefore, without committing himself to all the vagaries of pragmatic philosophy, . . . safely say, that at the present time most students regard the postulation of fundamental political principles of universal application as a statement of "mere useless opprobrious theory."[2]

And a few years later William Y. Elliott wrote that pragmatism "has been the main stream of American political science."[3]

The preoccupation with finding the proper "method" for the new science, which is evident in the various writings of those early days, although attributable in general to the success of the physical sciences in the latter half of the nineteenth century, must be attributed specifically to pragmatic philosophy. This, too, was of German origin, derived as it was from the philosophy of Kant and Hegel,[4] but it reached America by a different route and its influence on American political science was not entirely compatible with the influence of the German historical school.

Like the Prussian political science that so influenced Burgess and the first generation of American political scientists, pragmatism incorporated the doctrine of progress. But the doctrine took a somewhat different form. As Henry Steele Commager wrote, "It subscribed readily enough to the doctrine of progress, but made that doctrine contingent rather than absolute—contingent upon the contributions which men were willing to risk for its realization."[5] History was still thought to be unidirectional, but advances were not self-realizing: they depended upon application of the proper method.

Pragmatism is often treated in contemporary literature[6] merely as an expression of American culture. That is, pragmatism is treated as nothing more than a systematic version of the typical American quality of practicality[7] (or, in the writings of Bertrand Russell, as the theoretical expression of American capitalism). This is a fundamental misunderstanding.

Pragmatism was a definite school of thought, or of philosophy, the principles of which were first articulated in the writings of Charles Peirce, William James, and John Dewey. Like any school of thought, pragmatism comprises disagreements as well as certain fundamental points of agreement. Nevertheless, there is an "essential community of interest" among the various species of pragmatism, consisting of "a common protest against that intellectualism which regards the real world as the consummation of reason" and of a "complete repudiation of absolutism."

Pragmatism has been described as

> more an attitude of mind than a system of ideas; (the name] has been applied to many different, and often conflicting, systems. All such systems, however, have in common certain fundamentals, such as the plurality and diversity of things and thoughts, the primacy of change, movement and activity, the genuineness of novelty and belief in immediate experience as the court of last resort in validating ideas.[9]

And George Sabine wrote that "pragmatism" was

> a name or rather indefinite meaning, signifying a group of scientific and philosophical tendencies rather than a systematic doctrine. It does stand roughly for a point of view, which has perhaps been stated most

clearly by Professor John Dewey, and it is a fact that this point of view has acted as a sort of ferment outside philosophy especially in economics and law.[10]

Furthermore, pragmatism applied is not necessarily identical to pragmatism in theory. As the doctrine spread from its original expositors, especially Peirce, James, and Dewey, to become the regnant philosophy of American academia, what common identity it originally possessed was weakened.

Nor was the term "pragmatism" confined only to the pristine doctrine of its inventors, for it was one of several contending schools of thought that were combined or confounded in application. In its narrow sense, pragmatism was the philosophical doctrine taught at Harvard and Chicago. In a broader sense, pragmatism was part of what has been characterized as a "revolt against formalism" in late nineteenth- and early twentieth-century American thought. The form of pragmatism that so influenced American political science was, "in short, behavioristic in terms of psychology and positivistic in terms of philosophy."[11]

The development of pragmatism paralleled the development of anti-formalist (or, in Elliott's account, anti-intellectual[12]) schools of thought in history, economics, and law:

> Pragmatism, instrumentalism, institutionalism, economic determinism, and legal realism exhibit striking philosophical kinships. They are all suspicious of approaches which are excessively formal; they all protest their anxiety to come to grips with reality, their attachment to the moving and vital in social life. Most of those who founded or represented these movements started their serious thinking in the eighties and nineties of the last century, a period of ignition in American thought.[13]

Pragmatism shared with other aspects of the anti-formalist movement both "impatience with reason (as reason is expressed in metaphysics and logic)" and the "absence of principle, and of moral or other standards."[14]

Even on the question of the scope of scientific method, the main concern of this chapter, "individual pragmatists have not all been consistent . . . [and] the movement as a whole has been divided."[15] Nevertheless, among the three leading pragmatists of the late nineteenth and early twentieth centuries there is a kind of consensus on what the method is. It is that consensus, rather than the disagreement about the scope of its possible application, that influenced the founders of academic political science.

Pragmatism denies all possibility of objective knowledge of the external world. Rejecting the classical (and Enlightenment) position that there is a real world independent of man's apprehension or understanding of it, and that our understanding more or less closely approaches the truth about that world, pragmatism redefines "truth" so as to make it a concept independent of any externally existing reality. The problem of epistemology, of the adequacy of man's perception of the universe in which he dwells, is thus finessed. For pragmatism, what is true is not what coincides with reality but what forms a usable whole.

William James, even while insisting that pragmatism did not deny the existence of the real world, distinguished pragmatism from other forms of positivism in respect of differing attitudes toward the meaning of "truth."[16] According to James, positivism treated truth as an objectively existing relationship between the real world and statements about the real world, and thus, for positivism, the truth of a statement was independent of its empirical verification or verifiability. Pragmatism, on the other hand, defined "truth" as verification (or verifiability); "truth," for the pragmatist, simply meant the verification process.[17] As Elliott wrote, "Absolute truth [James] renounced cheerfully in favor of that 'working truth' which his psychological insight showed him that men accepted and lived upon."[18]

The pragmatic conception of truth was the foundation of the doctrine that James himself referred to as "radical empiricism." That doctrine excluded from philosophic discourse any consideration of objects other than as defined by our experience of them.[19] The individual character of experience poses a problem for James's radical empiricism; as A. J. Ayer put it, it is "the problem of explaining how the contents of the experiences of different people can serve to construct a common world."[20] To this problem the pragmatists, and James in particular, had no satisfactory answer, although, as it turns out, the quest for pragmatic truth is very much a collective endeavor.

The innovation of pragmatism was its reliance upon method, or, in contemporary language, "methodology." A statement could be said to be true or false only as it "worked" or did not "work." There had, therefore, to be a test of workability, a method by which the utility of a statement could be evaluated. The only way in which pragmatism could "avoid introducing a normative element or a coherent groundwork of logic into its system" was by accepting the full implications of a positivistic method, i.e., by the attempt to find a completely satisfactory account of knowledge and of value in a description of what are called "the facts" of a given specific situation.[21]

Because the truth or falsehood of putative knowledge is not determinable by either internal or external tests, the functional substitute is evaluation of the method by which the data were obtained. A community of scholars was a community constituted and given identity by its methodology. This is an example of what has been called "the illusion of technique,"[22] the modernist exaltation of process over substance.

The word "truth" itself was appropriated to refer to the body of findings according to the appropriate method at any given time; the word was held to have no significance outside of the method or over the passage of time. "True ideas," said William James, "are those that we can assimilate, validate, corroborate and verify. False ideas are those that we cannot."[23] Truth was understood as a quality shared by many ideas and opinions, in respect of their usefulness or their verifiability: "Our account of truth is an account of truths in the plural, of processes of leading, realized *in rebus* and having only this quality in common, that they pay," wrote James, and, "Truth for us is simply a collective name for verification-processes."[24]

The "truth" about a particular subject was the consensus of the practitioners of the science of that subject, and was, therefore, another name for opinion. It was not that the divided line was united, rather that it was truncated at its division. Genuine knowledge being unattainable there is only opinion, and opinion founded upon the proper method is rebaptized "knowledge." John Dewey, for example, defined "knowledge" as "belief authorized by inquiry."[25]

But the scientist is motivated by his desire to solve particular problems within his particular field and by his desire to predict and control outcomes. Pragmatism

accepts control as the end of knowledge and the test of its efficacy, and thus makes purpose an ineradicable part of all thinking. It acknowledges only an *ad hoc* test of truth, since thinking must succeed, if at all, only in terms of the problem that calls it forth.[26]

The "end" and "purpose" here are as much matters of opinion as the "knowledge." They are either matters of unguided human choice or are dictated by historical conditions. Hence, Sabine wrote that for the pragmatist "a theorist ought to be as self-conscious and as methodical about purposes as about facts,"[27] although he "obviously must not . . . confuse purposes with facts."[28]

The pragmatists thought themselves in a "universe of change and uncertainty."[29] The doctrine of evolution popularized by Charles Darwin had suggested a "process of endless change, without fixed ends, in which the course of change could be plotted only for limited intervals and in terms of causal relationships having a rather limited span."[30] The emergence of the doctrine of evolution formed, for the pragmatists, the pivotal point of the history of ideas. Not only biology, but science, philosophy, and politics were transformed:

> Yet after all we need only recur to the science of plants and animals as it was before Darwin and to the ideas which even now are dominant in moral and political matters to find the older order of conceptions in full possession of the popular mind. Until the dogma of fixed unchangeable types and species, of arrangement in classes of higher and lower, of subordination of the transitory individual to the universal or kind had been shaken in its hold upon the science of life, it was impossible that the new ideas and methods should be made at home in social and moral life. Does it not seem to be the intellectual task of the twentieth century to take this last step?[31]

The doctrine of evolution applied, according to the pragmatists, not only to plant and animal species, not only to political life, but to truth itself. "[W]e have to live today by what truth we can get today," wrote James, "and be ready tomorrow to call it falsehood."[32] Their concern, therefore, was "with the integrity and durability of inquiry, on the one hand, and the tentativeness, falibility, and incompleteness of knowledge on the other,"[33] and it was to "what they called the 'spirit' of science, or its 'method' and 'attitude' that they looked for a foundation stable enough to support a modern culture."[34] Peirce, James, Dewey, and their followers therefore stressed "the priority of method as a cultural commitment."[35]

The method favored by the pragmatists led to definition of things not according to their nature or their inherent properties, but according to how they behaved when a series of experiments was performed upon them. Because the influence of pragmatism upon the infant academic discipline of political science was preeminently in giving that method to the discipline, it is worthwhile to see how the method applied to the realm of natural science. The application of the method yields results which are predictive, rather than normative. The prototype of the pragmatic method is Charles Peirce's definition of lithium:

> If you search among minerals that are vitreous, translucent, grey or white, very hard, brittle, and insoluable, for one which imparts a crimson tinge to an unluminous flame, this mineral being triturated with lime or witherite rats-bane, and then fused, can be partly dissolved in muriatic acid; and if this solution be evaporated, and the residue be extracted with sulphuric acid, and duly purified, it can be converted by ordinary methods into a chloride, which being obtained in the solid state, fused, and electrolyzed with a half dozen powerful cells, will yield a globule of pinkish silvery metal that will float on gasolene; and the material of *that* is a specimen of lithium.[36]

John Dewey used a similar, if homelier, example to illustrate the same point. He wrote:

> To judge that this object is sweet, that is, to refer the idea or meaning "sweet" to it without actually experiencing sweetness, is to predict that when tasted—that is, subjected to a specified operation—a certain consequence will ensue.[37]

The method described requires the scientist to be an active agent in the process of definition, rather than an observer only. A thing is not satisfactorily defined until it is tortured—burnt, bent, beaten, dissolved in acid, centrifuged, consumed, devoured. There is no reason to suppose that the method would change much when applied to human concerns. Indeed, behavioral political and social science is just that method applied to politics and society.

An academic discipline constituted, for Charles Peirce and the other pragmatists, "an eternally self-correcting community of inquiry."[38] So subjective an understanding of what it means for a statement to be true as that advanced by the pragmatists would seem to point in the direction of solipsism. A shared, professional appreciation of what works in a given field is a functional substitute for objective knowledge. As the intellectual historian Thomas Haskell wrote:

> [T]he very existence of a community of inquiry was a guarantee against intellectual chaos, because the community's current best opinion was the closest approach to the truth that mankind could ever hope to achieve in practice.[39]

The community, i.e. in fact the academic discipline, was to be self-identifying and self-correcting. One scholar has said of the community of inquiry:

> The great functional advantage of the disciplined community of inqury over unorganized individual inquirers is that the community, by its very existence, supplies mankind with indirect criteria of credibility and authority. It provides a practical way of recognizing (probable) sound opinion when that opinion cannot be directly checked against "the truth." Deprived of self-evident truth, unable to trust tradition, modern man has no other recourse, Peirce seems to have believed, than the consensus of the competent. Sound opinion becomes that opinion which wins the broadest and deepest support in the existing community of inquiry: there is, according to Peirce, no higher test of reality.[40]

American political science, and especially the American Political Science Association during its early years, rapidly came to recognize itself as a Peircean "community of inquiry." The views of the A.P.S.A. membership (and they were remarkably homogeneous) represented the consensus of the competent on questions of public affairs.

The essential element of pragmatism was the "willingness to treat knowledge as temporal and to treat method as both primary and enduring."[41] Opinion was knowledge, was true, if it was useful, and ceased to be true when it ceased to be useful. William James wrote:

> You can say of [such an opinion] then either that "it is useful because it is true" or that "it is true because it is useful." Both these phrases mean exactly the same thing, namely that here is an idea that gets fulfilled and can be verified.[42]

The utility that was equated to truth was utility in further inquiry. According to James:

> [P]ossession of true thoughts means everywhere possession of invaluable instruments of action. The possession of truth, so far from being here an end in itself, is only a preliminary means towards other vital satisfactions.[43]

Pragmatism, as Henry Steele Commager wrote, "made philosophy a servant, not a master, an instrument, not an end."[44]

Pragmatism, in one form or another shaped the "main stream" of American political science. Elliott asserted:

> At least one side of pragmatism, with its insistence upon the concrete and the immediate, is an encouragement to this much business, a defence of the assumption that general theory is irrelevant, and an apologia for the method of purely scientific description as the only approach to politics.[45]

The "scientific" political scientist, under that influence, tried to describe political phenomena "without ethical or metaphysical bias if he were to qualify as a true scientist."[46] As a result of that attitude, he would attempt to treat "social phenomena as if reason and a normative human will did not exist" in them, adopting a methodological "skepticism of rational purpose in politics."[47]

Commager, describing the movement "toward a new science of politics" asserted:

> The pragmatic approach had more direct and immediate consequences even than the evolutionary. For where evolution was a philosophical attitude, pragmatism was a technique; where evolution furnished a point of departure pragmatism required analysis and solution.[48]

Commager, of course, used "pragmatic" more broadly than it has been used in this chapter, but the point is valid nonetheless. The result of this influence was that the new political scientists "called all political institutions into their laboratories and subjected them to scientific tests."[49] The pervasiveness of the influence is indicated by Commager's comment that the "pragmatists did not so much constitute a school as a whole eductional system."[50] In this group, he put A. L. Lowell, Henry Jones Ford, Woodrow Wilson, Charles E. Merriam, W. F. Willoughby, and Frank J. Goodnow.

Pragmatism, or at least a version of pragmatism emphasizing the community of inquiry and the primacy of methodology, was an important influence on the professionalization of American political science. But it was not only in the organization of the discipline and the quest for an appropriate method that pragmatism was influential. Many, perhaps most, of the new political scientists were also political activists. Pragmatism not only contributed to the shaping of the discipline and its methods but also suggested applications of the new political science to the practical world of politics.

Pragmatism was not politically neutral, but entailed a commitment to democracy and socialism. John Dewey attributed his interest in the interaction of social conditions with scientific and philosophic thought to the influence of Auguste Comte,[51] and he condemned even such modern philosophers as John Locke for failing to articulate or apply the method implicit in natural science and democracy.[52] The unending process of inquiry applied not only to philosophy and science but to society itself. Politics was not to be based on fixed principles but on the experimental method. John Dewey's approach to moral and political science has been summarized as follows:

> [H]e declared that the only way in which ethical judgments could be confirmed was by the use of scientific method in the modern as opposed to the ancient sense. . . . The great problem for modern man, said Dewey, was to heal the breach between morals and science which had opened up after the medieval synthesis had broken down. This, he said, could be accomplished only by resting moral knowledge on science properly conceived. Armed with such knowledge, philosophers could participate in a great effort to make society over by applying science to individual conduct and to social institutions.[53]

Herbert D. Croly, Walter Lippman, and Walter E. Weyl were the polemicists of pragmatism under its political aspect, reflecting "precisely the combination of hopes and aspirations found in the classic texts of the pragmatist philosophers."[54] The essential fact for the success of that political program was that its adherents claimed for democracy and socialism the status of method rather than of principle.

The political program of the pragmatists, together with a variety of reform movements around the turn of the century, constitutes the third major intellectual influence on the founding of American academic political science: Progressivism. The influence of progressivism upon American political science will be treated in the next chapter; for the present it suffices to note the close connection between the two movements.

In the politics of the world rebuilding from the Great War and enduring the economic depression which the Great War brought on, the implications of pragmatism became more clear. While the original pragmatists were liberal, progressive, or socialist in their own politics, the fundamental assumptions of pragmatism led as well to other forms of politics. Elliott, tracing the political tendencies of pragmatist theory, found that "[i]n the end its functionalist attitude re-enthrones the state as an organic necessity, stripped of other than economic restraints,—in short, Fascism."[55]

There remains to be explored the effect of pragmatism on the emerging American academic discipline of political science—that is, to examine the effect of denial of the possibility of real knowledge of the external world combined with faith in scientific method and the community of inquiry, as well as acceptance of usefulness as the criterion for "truth," on the emerging American academic discipline of political science.

In the first place, the new approach liberated the new political scientists from the traditional ways of studying and teaching about politics. As George Sabine wrote:

> [T]he pragmatic method . . . offers a large degree of freedom from tradition, a deliverance from useless abstractions, and the possibility of harnessing logical operations—classification, deduction, and induction—to problems that will not let political theory get too far away from real situations.[56]

This liberation was especially apparent in terms of legal studies, where "the pragmatic method [was] directly opposed to the type of formal legal studies which have issued in the theory of sovereignty and the juristic theory of the state."[57]

Second, the search for the appropriate method for political science provided an air of authenticity to the new science. The application of scientific method was the guarantee of authenticity and of progress within an intellectual system which could not measure progress in terms of externally defined ends and which denied the possibility of genuine, objective knowledge of the world.

Third, because "for a brief period, the Progressive Era itself, pragmatism so coincided with a particular frame of mind and a particular politics"[58] that it united the professional scientific activity of the academic political scientist with the active political work of the social reformer. Knowledge, after all, was the product of experiment; a statement of fact was merely a prediction of the results of such experiment. Social reform was a kind of experiment available to test the hypotheses of the political scientist. Society itself was the matter to be heated, cooled, dissolved, centrifuged, and so forth.

Pragmatism as a school of thought (or of philosophy) became, during the first two decades of the present century, the American philosophy. It won the hearts and minds of American intellectuals, and, most especially, of American academics practicing the new, or newly reconceived, disciplines of political science, sociology, economics, and history. Bernard Crick accurately described the hegemony of pragmatism when he wrote that "[b]y the early 'twenties there was scarcely a social scientist who did not consider himself, in some sense, a pragmatist."[59]

NOTES

1. Frank J. Goodnow, *Social Reform and the Constitution* (New York: The Macmillan Company, 1911), 3.

2. Goodnow, *Social Reform*, 3–4.

3. William Y. Elliott, *The Pragmatic Revolt in Politics* (New York: The Macmillan Company, 1928), 7.

4. John Dewey, "The Development of American Pragmatism," *Revue de Metaphysique et de Morale* 47: 411–430, translated and reprinted in *An Anthology of Recent Philosophy*, ed. by Daniel S. Robinson (New York: Thomas Y. Crowell Company, 1929), 431–445.

5. Henry Steele Commager, *The American Mind: An Interpretation of American Thought and Culture since the 1880's* (New Haven, Conn.: Yale University Press, 1950), 96.

6. See David A. Hollinger, "The Problem of Pragmatism in American History," *The Journal of American History*, 67, no. 1 (1980): 88–92 and *passim*; Dewey, "Development of American Pragmatism," 431–433 and *passim*.

7. This is emphatically the case with the treatment of pragmatism in Commager's *American Mind*. (See especially chapter 5.)

8. Elliott, *Pragmatic Revolt*, 45.

9. Horace M. Kallen, "Pragmatism" in *Encyclopaedia of the Social Sciences*, ed. by E. R. A. Seligman (New York: The Macmillan Company, 1948), vol. 12, 307.

10. George H. Sabine, "The Pragmatic Approach to Politics," *The American Political Science Review*, vol. 24 (1930): 865.

11. Elliott, *Pragmatic Revolt*, 6.

12. Elliott, *Pragmatic Revolt*, 10.

13. Morton G. White, *Social Thought in America: The Revolt against Formalism* (Boston: Beacon Press, 1957), 6.

14. Elliott, *Pragmatic Revolt*, 5.

15. Morton G. White, "Pragmatism and the Scope of Science," in *Pragmatism and the American Mind* (New York: Oxford University Press, 1973), 109.

16. Commager, an unabashed admirer, referred to pragmatism not as a school of philosophy but as an "attitude toward truth" (94).

17. William James, *The Meaning of Truth: A Sequel to Pragmatism* (Ann Arbor: University of Michigan Press, 1970) 182–184. [Originally published in 1909.]

18. Elliott, *Pragmatic Revolt*, 23.

19. A. J. Ayer, *The Origins of Pragmatism* (San Francisco: Freeman, Cooper & Company, 1968), 215–216.

20. Ayer, *Origins of Pragmatism*, 220.

21. Elliott, *Pragmatic Revolt*, 24.

22. William Barrett, *The Illusion of Technique* (New York: Doubleday, 1978), xi–xvi.

23. William James, "Pragmatism's Conception of Truth," Lecture 6 of *Pragmatism: A New Name for Some Old Ways of Thinking* (1907), reprinted in *Essays in Pragmatism*, Alburey Eastell, ed. (New York: Hafner Publishing Co., 1948), 160.

24. James, "Pragmatism's Conception of Truth," 168.

25. John Dewey, "Science as Subject-Matter and as Method," *Science*, vol. 31 (1910), 121–127, at 125.

26. Sabine, "Pragmatic Approach to Politics," 866–867.

27. Sabine, "Pragmatic Approach to Politics," 881.

28. Sabine, "Pragmatic Approach to Politics," 881.

29. Hollinger, "Problem of Pragmatism," 93.

30. Sabine, "Pragmatic Approach to Politics," 866.

31. John Dewey, *Reconstruction in Philosophy* (New York: New American Library, 1950), 76. [Originally published in 1920.]

32. James, "Pragmatism's Conception of Truth," 170.

33. Hollinger, "Problem of Pragmatism," 93.

34. Hollinger, "Problem of Pragmatism," 93.

35. Hollinger, "Problem of Pragmatism," 94.

36. Charles S. Pierce, quoted in Morton G. White, *Science and Sentiment in America: Philosophical Thought from Jonathan Edwards to John Dewey* (New York: Oxford University Press, 1972), 154.

37. John Dewey, quoted in White, *Science and Sentiment*, 274.

38. Hollinger, "Problem of Pragmatism," 95.

39. Thomas L. Haskell, *The Emergence of Professional Social Science: The American Social Science Association and the Nineteenth-Century Crisis of Authority* (Urbana, Ill.: University of Illinois Press, 1977), 108.

40. Haskell, *Emergence*, 239.

41. Hollinger, "Problem of Pragmatism," 95.

42. James, "Pragmatism's Conception of Truth," 163.

43. James, "Pragmatism's Conception of Truth," 161.

44. Commager, *American Mind*, 95.

45. Elliott, *Pragmatic Revolt*, 7.

46. Elliott, *Pragmatic Revolt*, 8.

47. Elliott, *Pragmatic Revolt*, 9.

48. Commager, *American Mind*, 325.

49. Commager, *American Mind*, 326.

50. Commager, *American Mind*, 326.

51. White, *Science and Sentiment*, 269.
52. White, *Science and Sentiment*, 270.
53. White, *Science and Sentiment*, 273.
54. Hollinger, "Problem of Pragmatism," 103.
55. Elliott, *Pragmatic Revolt*, 31.
56. Sabine, "Pragmatic Approach to Politics," 885.
57. Sabine, "Pragmatic Approach to Politics," 880.
58. Bernard Crick, *The American Science of Politics: Its Origin and Conditions* (Berkeley: University of California Press, 1959), 88.
59. Crick, *American Science*, 88.

Chapter Three

PROGRESSIVISM

The Progressive movement has been aptly defined as "the general movement of reform . . . aimed at making government, Municipal, State or National, both more democratic and more efficient."[1] Although, as one historian has written, "progressivism was not one movement but many, each of its adherents having different immediate objects, often in conflict with the objects of the others,"[2] those movements can be said to have represented a sustained effort to achieve a number of political reforms. For a time, between the turn of the twentieth century and the First World War, Progressivism dominated the American political scene.

There seems to have been a general feeling, in the wake of the urbanization and industrialization of much of America, that the citizens had lost control of the country. Economic life had come to be dominated by large corporations; the cities were in the hands of the bosses and the machines. A series of political reforms seemed to be required, to reinvigorate democracy and to make it more efficient. Not everyone who could be characterized as a Progressive advocated all of them, but everyone who could be so characterized advocated some of them.

The specific political reforms of the era have been enumerated by historians:

Electoral changes appeared in rapid-fire order. The secret Australian
ballot, which enabled the voter to cast his ballot in private, insured his
independence from "machine" pressures at the polls. Direct primaries
removed the nomination of party candidates from a convention controlled by party workers and placed it in the hands of the voters. Sena-
torial elections, formerly the province of state legislators who seemed
distressingly susceptible to outside influences, came under popular control in the Seventeenth Amendment, adopted in 1913. The initiative,
referendum, and recall, which involved legislation by direct popular
will, became far more controversial. . . . Cities and states adopted por-
tions of the "Oregon system." . . . Agitation for woman suffrage also
increased rapidly.[3]

But the movement, as an intellectual phenomenon, began somewhat
earlier. The Progressive political sentiment has been characterized in a
single sentence by Arthur Link, one of the movement's leading historians: "By 1900 the ideal of an individualistic society had given way, at
least in the minds of many intellectuals and political leaders, to the
concept of a society organized for collective action in the public interest."[4] Link, in characterizing the intellectual and political impulses he is
describing, uses the word "reform" almost interchangeably with "Progressive."[5] The impulse toward reform was the hallmark of the movement and the era.

Another historian has characterized the "ideology of progress" that
was the creed of the political scientists who invented the new science of
politics in the first two decades of the twentieth century as follows:
"Continuous progress would result from consciously directed, continuous
revolution, and politics would be progressively freed from tragedy and
sorrow."[6] That is as much a characterization of the politicians and
intellectuals whose movement we call "Progressive" as of the founders
of academic political science. "Most progressive thinkers," another
historian has written, believed "that evolution could be controlled and
accelerated to bring about social justice, perhaps in their lifetime."[7] The
overlapping of the sentiments of the two groups mirrors the overlapping
of the membership of the two groups. A study of the period reveals how
"much of the Progressive literature was written by a first generation of
academic . . . specialists, in what was beginning to be known as political
science."[8]

Progressivism was the closest thing to an official ideology within the
American academic community—or at least within the new departments

of political and social science. In a way, the "universities demonstrated what other progressive ideas meant in practice. American universities were committed to research, practical service, and, sometimes, liberal culture. In the Progressive Era they were also supposed to advance democracy."[9] What they did advance, of course, was the "new" social thought of Progressive intellectuals.

The ideal was expressed in the title of Woodrow Wilson's inaugural address as president of Princeton University: "Princeton in the Nation's Service." The Progressive intellectuals who founded and led the new universities spoke of them as national resources, as centers of social service. "Within the university," as one historian has pointed out,

> the call to social service produced important results. Semiautonomous "schools" of political science came into being at Columbia in 1880, at Michigan the next year, and at Wisconsin in 1892; and a special "course" of this nature was established at Cornell.[10]

It is hardly surprising that the greatest part of the "social service" enterprise within the university should be concentrated in the school of political science.

> The "radical" social scientists naturally found positions at the semiautonomous "schools" of political science which White among others had promoted with great vigor. And they understandably flocked to the universities where a utilitarian educational faith was conspicuously in evidence.[11]

The schools of political science thus became the home of the "new social thought" of the Progressive Era.

> The new social thought did not believe in natural laws that explained all behavior, but in constantly changing processes. Most critics of laissez faire believed that these processes could be understood and manipulated so that progress could be willed rather than just awaited. . . . Through what John Dewey termed "creative intelligence" and others called "practical idealism" they would build the kind of society that before them people had only dreamed of.[12]

Dewey, the pragmatist philosopher, sought to systematize that belief, to turn it into a metaphysical doctrine; for others it was sufficient as a general attitude toward the world. "Progressive intellectuals generally agreed with Dewey that society was plastic, change inevitable, and creative intelligence the way to guide it."[13]

The Progressive movement was unique among protest movements. It arose in a time of prosperity, and it arose among the middle and upper middle classes.[14] Historians of the movement agree that the leaders of the Progressive movement "were anything but bushy-bearded radicals."[15] Instead, most "were college graduates and, as members of the professions or owners of businesses had positions of importance."[16] A historian of the California movement found that the typical Progressive leader "held a significant niche in the American economic structure. . . . While not wealthy, the average California progressive was, in the jargon of the day, 'well fixed,'" and, as a group, the Progressive leaders were "highly literate, independent free enterprisers and professional men."[17] In the Midwest, too, Progressive leadership "came not from the uncombed third-party groups," but, instead, from "smart young Republican lawyers, district attorneys, and young career politicians" who were "sharp, well educated, efficient, and practical men."[18] The movement was the creature of an elite that included independent businessmen, young professionals, and, especially, intellectuals.

The relationship of the Progressive movement to the intellectual community, more especially to the universities, and most especially to the emerging social sciences, was a key to its success. One historian of the Progressive movement gave his chapter on that relationship the title "The Capture of the Ivory Tower" and set it as the center of his book.[19] He described the new social sciences, and especially their professional organizations, as organs of the Progressive ideology:

> Before 1880 there were practically no systematic research techniques employed in the social sciences. . . . However, a whole new group of social theorists appeared, many of them trained in Germany. They founded new organizations for the exchange of information and to attack social and economic problems from a new viewpoint—the American Historical Association, the American Economic Association, the American Political Science Association, the American Sociological Association, and others. What they had to say squared not at all with the older prevailing theories.[20]

The Progressive movement, of which the reform impulse was the major political expression, was a reaction to the closing of the frontier (as Wilson's friend and Johns Hopkins classmate pointed out in a famous essay) and to "the profound cultural crisis caused by the rapid urbanization and industrialization of the nation during the nineteenth century."[21] Historians like George Bancroft had portrayed American history as a pageant of continuing progress in the amelioration of man's estate and in the advance of scientific knowledge. The rise of cities and factories, attended by slums, labor unrest, and political corruption, seemed to mark the end of that progress. One historian of Progressive thought has described this crisis of cultural confidence:

> [U]ntil the 1880s most Americans could define national history as progress in the sense that the destruction of slavery and the slavocracy was a purge, eliminating cultural complexity and restoring national simplicity. Recognition of the prsence of the factory, the city, and the corporation came as a terrible shock, therefore, in the 1880s. . . . Throughout the entire material culture in the 1880s there appeared expressions of the fear that the nation had begun the downward path of cultural decadence.[22]

The Progressive intellectuals, however, saw in urbanization and industrialization an opportunity more than a threat. The primary reinterpreters of these phenomena were the journalists and social critics Herbert D. Croly, Walter E. Weyl, and Walter Lippman. Weyl, for example, wrote:

> Individualism struck its frontier when the pioneer struck his, and society, falling back on itself, found itself. New problems arose, requiring for their solution slight amendments of our former canons of judgment and modes of action. . . . In obedience to this new spirit we are slowly changing our perception and evaluation of the goods of life. . . . The inner soul of our new democracy is not the unalienable rights, negatively and individualistically interpreted, but those same rights, "life, liberty, and the pursuit of happiness," extended and given a social interpretation.[23]

But, at the turn of the century one of the junior members of the faculty Burgess had assembled at the Columbia School of Political Science also emerged as a Progressive theorist. That was Charles A. Beard, a student under Goodnow of public administration and municipal government, who had also studied in Britain and Germany. "His European experiences in the 1890s prepared Beard to become a prophet of the Progressive moment when Americans escaped the feeling of aging and decadence and regained the sense of youthful vigor."[24]

Beard was among the first of the academic political scientists to put his "scientific" pursuits in the service of political action. Academic propriety and the attempt to see politics from the viewpoint of the neutral, disinterested observer kept his colleagues from committing themselves to partisan action, but to Beard it seemed

> inevitable that industrialism would produce a greater democracy in America than ever existed before. It was unscientific, therefore, for scholars to defend the status quo. To be truly objective, they would have to demonstrate those factors which would inexorably bring about a cooperative democracy.[25]

In works including *The Industrial Revolution* (1901) and *An Economic Interpretation of the Constitution* (1913), as well as his lecture on "Politics" (1908),

> Beard was rewriting American history so that the national identity as a democracy of free and equal producers lay in the future and not in the past. He stressed the undemocratic nature of the Republic in 1789 and . . . argued [that Americans] must reject an undemocratic political system based on eighteenth-century aristocratic principles.[26]

One of the first objects of reform during the early Progressive Era was municipal government. In the campaign for municipal reform, academic political scientists took a leading part, including

> their very influential role in shaping the agenda of the national reform movement. Present at the creation of the National Municipal League in 1894, these academics succeeded in gradually shifting its focus from reportage to prescriptive analysis. When the League's Municipal Program was unveiled in 1899, it bore the clear stamp of the new poltical science. Its drafting had been dominated by Goodnow, his students John Fairlie and Delos Wilcox, Wilson's classmate Albert Shaw, and Leo Rowe of the University of Pennsylvania.[27]

Beard, "a loyal disciple of Goodnow," was among those Goodnow interested in the cause of municipal reform; that influence is evident in Beard's *American City Government* (1912).[28]

Although it was not only municipal government that was in need of reform, it was on that level that the reformist impulse began to have a great influence. The municipal reform movement began in the 1870s, but was integrated into Progressivism. Thereafter, political reform, along the lines of the earlier municipal reform, became a part of the movement's credo. Municipal reformers had sought to put government upon a scientific basis and to replace political appointees with nonpartisan experts. As Dwight Waldo has summarized it, this "growing current of thought became a part of Progressivism, and upon the advent of the First Great War, Science was a cult and Expert a fetish."[29]

One of the best statements of the relationship of this Progressivism to American political science was made in Woodrow Wilson's presidential address to the American Political Science Association in 1911. The address was entitled "The Law and the Facts"[30] and in it Wilson set forth a Progressive theory of law and of political science. Law, Wilson argued, "records life. . . . It is subsequent to fact and it takes its origin and energy from the actual circumstances of social experience."[31] In Progressive society law changes constantly as the society itself evolves; some laws, of reformist tendency, may apparently anticipate and direct the changes in society itself. Wilson defined political science as:

> the accurate and detailed observation of these processes by which the lessons of experience are brought into the field of consciousness, transmuted into active purposes, put under the scrutiny of discussion, sifted, and at last given determinate form in law.[32]

Political science constantly becomes more complex, even as society itself becomes more complex; and progress consists in movement from the relatively simple to the complex. In America, seen as a modern, complex society, society and law have experienced "a rapid development of individual forces" constituting "a great spectacle of force released and challenged," resulting in legislation that was "atomistic, miscellaneous, piecemeal, makeshift." Therefore, the "elusive, complex, yet imperative task of political science" is to bring about the "adjustment, synthesis, coordination, harmony, and union" of the laws—that is of the experience of society itself—into a systematic whole. Political scientists, indeed, the members of the A.P.S.A., were to be "a self-constituted commission" to bring that systematic whole into existence.

The necessity of guiding change follows from the increasing complexity of the society and from the increasing number of forces at work in society. "The processes of change will be organic only in proportion as they are guided and framed along self-consistent lines of general policy."[33] The necessity is dictated by the process of evolution itself, for as "experience becomes more and more aggregate, law must be more and more organic, institutional, constructive."[34]

In the same address, Wilson outlined the Progressive conception of private economic activity: "society is the senior partner in all business." Business, that is, private enterprises, are to be "correlated, tamed, and harnessed" by political science. "Business," Wilson argued, "is no longer in any sense a private matter." In a sense, then, political science is in the service of subordinating private interests to collective, social interests.

Insofar as a coherent theory of Progressivism can be identified, the essential element of that theory is the doctrine of directed progress. "The distinguishing thing about the Progressives," one sympathetic historian has written, was not belief in progress but "something else, which for lack of a better term might be called 'activism.'" The author goes on to explain that the Progressives "believed that the people of the country should be stimulated to work energetically to bring about social progress."[35] "Social progress was not to be realized by sitting and praying, but by using the active powers; in short, by a revivification of democracy."[36]

Progressivism shared with professional political science two main themes or interests. The first was the critique of the Constitution of the United States[37] and the second was the separation of administration from politics.[38] Central to the Progressive theory of politics was the demand for the strengthening of the executive branch of government, that it should cease to be a "mere executive" and should become a government in the English sense, associated with, if not dominant in, the field of policy making, a demand that strengthened the feeling that only the elected members of the "executive" should be involved in policy decisions, leaving appointed officials to put these decisions into effect with impartial, expert efficiency.[39]

Along with the notion that democracy should consist in giving the fullest expression to the immediate will of the majority, Progressive thought advanced the notion that the administrative agencies were properly the agents of democracy. "The time has now come," wrote Herbert Croly in *Progressive Democracy*, "to consider the proper function of administrative agencies in the realization of a progressive democratic polity."[40] That proper function Croly laid out as follows:

> The sincere intention of such a democracy to promote individual and social welfare would give continuity to its policy and enable profitable lessons to be drawn from its experiments; but if any such result is to be accomplished, it must provide an appropriate agency for the work. The only agency which could be organized and equipped for its accom-

plishment would be a permanent body of experts in social administration.[41]

The need for a trained body of administrators was one that the new science of politics could help to fill. Even before Croly wrote, a succession of presidents of the American Political Science Association had offered the association's members, and their presumed scientific expertise, as a repository of facts and techniques to be used in the quest for more efficient government. Within the new discipline, public administration was the dominant specialization.

The species of the doctrine of historical progress introduced into America by adherents of the German science of politics posited a more or less automatic operation of impersonal forces. Political progress depended upon the genetic characteristics of various peoples and of their succession over time. It was inevitable that the Teutonic people, as the most political of peoples, should develop the idea of the national state, the most "modern," or advanced, form of political organization. The desirability of the national state was simultaneously defined and demonstrated by its position at the end, or, at any rate, at the latest point, of an evolutionary process.

The doctrine of progress inherent in pragmatist thought does not hold that progress is inevitable, but rather that it flows automatically from the application of a particular method, denominated the "scientific" method, to the material world. The method serves to guarantee that the result of the operation, if correctly performed, is progress.

Progressivism represents yet a third version of the doctrine of historical progress. In this version, progress depends upon the implementation of certain institutional reforms. This was as much a practical as a theoretical conclusion. Laissez-faire had not produced national progress because, left to their own devices, men pursue different aims with different degrees of ambition, luck, and skill. The result of a century and a half of laissez-faire was that some men became very rich while others were relatively poor. The disparity in economic resources resulted in a disparity of power. Therefore, as Herbert D. Croly wrote:

The automatic fulfillment of the American national Promise is to be abandoned, if at all, precisely because the traditional American confidence in individual freedom has resulted in a morally and socially undesirable distribution of wealth.[42]

Virtually the whole Progressive program, however, was oriented to means. Croly's "promise of American life" was a promise of procedure without content. Weyl's "new democracy" was meant as a seizing of power without a notion of what the power was to be used for.

In this emphasis on procedure, the Progressive impulse comes closest to the German historical school of politics. For the German academics, it was sufficient that the national state be brought into existence and that it exist in all its comprehensiveness; what it was to do, beyond the perfection and perpetuation of its existence, was not a matter of academic discussion. Similarly, for the Progressives, it was sufficient that political institutions become more democratic and efficient—that is, more responsive to the immediate political will of a simple numerical majority—it was apparently unnecessary thereafter to consider what actual measures might be adopted and efficiently carried out.

Progressivism, one historian has written, "simply meant that the rule of the majority should be expressed in a stronger government, one with a broader social and economic program and one more responsive to popular control." Democratic procedure was to be a guarantee of the results, a guarantee that one historian has expressed, not inappropriately, in religious terms:

> Under the influence of Darwinism, the rising social sciences, and a seemingly benign world, the progressive had traded some of his old mystical religion for a new social faith. He was aware that evil still existed, but he believed it a man-made thing and upon earth. What man created he could also destroy, and his present sinful state was the result of his conditioning. . . . The progressive, then, not only wanted to abolish a supernatural hell; he was intent upon secularizing heaven.[44]

The same historian goes on to quote an unidentified Progressive as writing, "The way to have a golden age is to elect it by an Australian [i.e., secret] ballot."[45]

NOTES

1. E. M. Hugh-Jones, *Woodrow Wilson and American Liberalism* (New York: Collier Books, 1962), 57.

2. Forrest McDonald, *The United States in the Twentieth Century* (Reading, Mass., and Menlo Park, Calif.: Addison-Wesley Publishing Company, 1970), vol. 1, 1900–1920, 61.

3. Samuel P. Says, *The Response to Industrialism: 1885–1914* (Chicago: University of Chicago Press, 1957), 155–156.

4. Arthur S. Link, *Woodrow Wilson and the Progressive Era: 1910–1917* (New York: Harper & Row, 1954), 1.

5. Link, *Woodrow Wilson*, 1–24, *passim*.

6. Thomas B. Silver, *Coolidge and the Historians* (Durham, N.C.: Carolina Academic Press, 1983), 2.

7. William L. O'Neill, *The Progressive Years: America Comes of Age* (New York: Dodd, Mead & Company, 1975), 95.

8. Michael H. Frisch, "Urban Theorists, Urban Reform, and American Political Culture in the Progressive Period," *Political Science Quarterly*, 97, no. 2 (Summer 1982): 297.

9. O'Neill, *Progressive Years*, 99.

10. Laurence R. Veysey, *The Emergence of the American University* (Chicago: University of Chicago Press, 1965), 72.

11. Veysey, *Emergence*, 74.

12. O'Neill, *Progressive Years*, 94.

13. O'Neill, *Progressive Years*, 105.

14. Charles Forcey, *The Crossroads of Liberalism: Croly, Weyl, Lippman, and the Progressive Era, 1900–1925* (New York: Oxford University Press, 1961), xi–xiii.

15. Forcey, *Crossroads*, xiii.

16. Forcey, *Crossroads*, xiii.

17. George E. Mowry, *The California Progressives* (Chicago: Quadrangle Books, 1963), 87–88.

18. Russell B. Nye, *Midwestern Progressive Politics: A History of Its Origins and Development, 1870–1958* (New York: Harper & Row, 1965), 183. [Originally published in East Lansing: Michigan State University Press, 1959.]

19. Nye, *Midwestern*, 125 *et seq.*

20. Nye, *Midwestern*, 137.

21. David W. Noble, *The Progressive Mind, 1890–1917* (Chicago: Rand-McNally & Co., 1970), 1.

22. Noble, *Progressive Mind*, 3–4.

23. Walter E. Weyl, *The New Democracy* (New York: Harper & Row, Publishers, 1964), 161. [Photographic reproduction of the first edition, published by Macmillan in 1912.]

24. Noble, *Progressive Mind*, 27.

25. Noble, *Progressive Mind*, 29.

26. Noble, *Progressive Mind*, 31.

27. Frisch, "Urban Theorists," 303.

28. Frisch, "Urban Theorists," 314.

29. Dwight Waldo, *The Administrative State: A Study of the Political Theory of American Public Administration* (New York: The Ronald Press, 1948), 29.

30. Woodrow Wilson, "The Law and the Facts," *American Political Science Review* 5, no. 1 (1911): 1–11.

31. Wilson, "Law and Facts," 1.

32. Wilson, "Law and Facts," 2.

33. Wilson, "Law and Facts," 9.

34. Wilson, "Law and Facts," 9.

35. Richard Hofstadter, "Introduction" to *The Progressive Movement, 1900–1915* (Englewood Cliffs, N.J.: Prentice-Hall, Inc., 1963), 4.

36. Hofstadter, "Introduction," 5.

37. See Chapter 5 below.

38. See Chapter 9 below.

39. M. J. C. Vile, *Constitutionalism and the Separation of Powers* (Oxford: Clarendon Press, 1967), 277.

40. Herbert Croly, *Progressive Democracy* (New York: The Macmillan Company, 1914), 349–350.

41. Croly, *Progressive Democracy*, 359.

42. Herbert Croly, *The Promise of American Life* (Indianapolis: The Bobbs-Merrill Company, Inc., 1965), 22. [Photographic reproduction of the original edition published by Macmillan in 1909.]

43. Nye, "Midwestern," 183.

44. Mowry, *California Progressives*, 98.

45. Mowry, *California Progressives*, 99.

Part II

THE OLD POLITICAL SCIENCE

Chapter Four

POLITICAL PHILOSOPHY

Political philosophy is the attempt to move from opinion to knowledge about the nature of the political things.[1] The founders of the new American political science did not believe in the possibility of knowledge superior to opinion about political things, or, perhaps more accurately, did not believe it possible to distinguish between opinion and knowledge about the political things. And they did not investigate the nature of political things, because that suggested a standard beyond their own concern and control. The founders of the new discipline concerned themselves with "the facts," their method was inductive; political philosophy seemed to be an attempt to go beyond "the facts" or to evade "the facts" or, possibly, to interpret "the facts" in order to suit predetermined ideas.

The new American political science constituted itself as a historical discipline, finding the facts of its subject in the historical and comparative study of political communities. In this respect, the new political science exhibited the characteristics attributed more generally to the dominant tendency of intellectual endeavor in the twentieth century:

It is no longer contemplative, but activistic; and it attaches to that study of the past which is guided by the anticipated future, or which starts

61

from and returns to the analysis of the present, a crucial philosophic significance: it expects from it the ultimate guidance for political life.[2]

Writing in 1925, Walter J. Shepard identified certain characteristics that marked the development of political science in the generation preceding his own. First among these was that "the historical method has clearly won general acceptance. Metaphysical, deductive, and analytical studies of the state have not entirely disappeared, but they have been pushed into the background."[3]

For political philosophy, nature is the standard against which actual politics is to be measured. For the new political science, history was that standard. In the writings of the founders of the new political science, as in the social sciences generally,

> [t]he questions of the modern state, of modern government, of the ideals of Western civilization, and so forth, occupy a place that was formerly occupied by the questions of the state and of the right way of life. Philosophic questions have been transformed into historical questions—or more precisely into historical questions of a "futuristic" character.[4]

Political philosophy was replaced by political history; and for courses in political philosophy were substituted such pale imitations as courses in the history of political ideas. Illustrative is the attitude of Raymond G. Gettell, who in *Problems in Political Evolution* took political theory as a datum of political history:

> The evolution of the state has followed two lines, fairly distinct, yet closely interrelated. One has been the development of the state in actual practice . . . The other . . . is the field of political theory . . . . Ordinarily, political theories are the direct result of objective political conditions. They reflect the thoughts and interpret the motives that underlie actual political development.[5]

The history of political institutions is the primary means of understanding political things. Not only did Gettell himself not attempt to understand politics theoretically, he saw the attempts of others to do so as reflections or rationalizations of political events. Although he was interested in finding "the general laws and principles upon which political development is based," Gettell was careful to warn against taking the generality of those laws or principles too seriously.[6] "History furnishes abundant evidence . . . to prove that the evolution of the state follows no universal sequences," but only general tendencies or directions.[7] Therefore, even political history cannot be generalized into theory, but rather particular "[p]olitical institutions can be understood only through a knowledge of their origin and past development."[8]

For Gettell, at least, political history was a consciously adopted substitute for political philosophy: "The intellectual point of view that considers the state a result of evolution is comparatively recent." The failure of "idealistic explanations," specifically including the doctrines of Aristotle, "cleared the way for those writers who looked to physical . . . forces, and who emphasized the importance of the natural environment, and of the economic factors underlying" social institutions.[9]

The doctrine, or ideology, of progress, in one or another or several of its forms, lies at the bottom of the new American political science. Humanity, culture, society, and politics are all, according to this doctrine, or this ideology, constantly evolving. Newer and older replace better and worse as analytical categories. Society becomes constantly more complex; and complexity is therefore itself a guarantee of progress. The more complex society becomes, the more government regulation is needed. Regulation is therefore also a guarantee that progress has occurred.

Three forms of the doctrine, or ideology, of progress have been described in the preceding chapters and their influence on and reflection in the new political science has been shown. The Prussian general state theory asserted that political communities evolve from the simple to the complex through a series of determinable stages, which stages are repeated in various societies at different times depending on the aptitude of the people for politics. The pragmatic emphasis on experimentation and description offered a methodology for progress, in politics as in other pursuits, by emphasizing "what works" over what is consistent with assumed principles. The progressive tendency toward political reform gave the new political science an agenda, and proceeded from the premise that progress could be accelerated by conscious manipulation.

The common element of the various forms of the doctrine of progress is the notion that there is no good or bad, only new and old. The idea of continuous advance implies that what is most advanced is most preferable, and is therefore to be sought. Political science might therefore consist of the identification of the direction of historical development. To know what is to be sought in politics, one must ask not "How ought we to be governed?" or "What end is to be served by politics?" but "What is

the next step in the process of development?" or "What is the next stage
of political evolution?"

A political science based on the question "What is the best form of
government?" is irrelevant once one has embraced the doctrine of
progress. Political philosophy, which asks such questions, is irrelevant;
but historical and comparative studies are relevant. Speculative political
theory is irrelevant, but experimental political science is relevant.

It is not surprising to find in the works of the founding generation of
the new political science a certain scorn and contempt for political
philosophy. John W. Burgess and Woodrow Wilson each dismissed the
airy speculation of political philosophers who imagined that they were
discovering immortal truths about the political things and who constructed pasts that never were to be the foundations of utopias that never
would be.

Westel W. Willoughby, although he called his major work *An
Examination of the* Nature *of the State* and who subtitled it *A Study in
Political Philosophy*, similarly disposed of past political philosophers.
His new political philosophy was in the way of being generalized
political history. So far from inquiring into the nature of the State, he
produced, as it were, a kind of *natural history* of the State.

History, more especially comparative political history, supplanted
political philosophy. And yet, there remained a kind of shadow of
political philosophy within the newly organizing discipline. One section
of the A.P.S.A., from the outset, was the section on Political Theory, last
ranked among the sections. The task of members of that section was to
preserve and discuss the political thought of the past, not to inquire into
whether political thinkers of the past had valuable insights for the
present, but as an antiquarian pursuit or as a way of disciplining the
mind. Political theory, like politics itself, was understood to be constantly evolving, Roman thought replacing Greek, medieval replacing
Roman, modern replacing medieval, and so on. The courses taught by
members of the Political Philosophy Section came to be courses in the
history of political thought.

The first version of the doctrine of progress to influence the new
American political science was a Hegelian version, imported with
academic political science itself from the nineteenth-century German
university. Robert Nisbet, in his *History of the Idea of Progress* wrote
concerning Hegel:

Progress is one sweeping force in Hegel's thought. . . . [The other] is the political state. . . . More successfully than any other philosopher in all Western history, Hegel united absolute faith in inexorable progress with equally absolute faith in the absolute political state.[10]

A second version was carried over from the school of philosophy called pragmatism, one of whose leading figures was John Dewey. As Nisbet wrote:

Dewey believed strongly in the uses of intellect for the purpose of rational, progressive reform. . . . [T]he whole point of what he and others called his "instrumentalism" was the utilization of thought and planning to supplement the natural processes of society and change. . . . [C]onfidence in natural progress underlies all of Dewey's manifestations of social reform, education, and morality.[11]

The third version of the doctrine of progress was that of the Progressive movement in politics. There were versions of this in both America and Europe. Nisbet summarized the two versions as follows:

In sum, whether in Europe or America, liberals old and new never doubted at least until recently that there was progress easily to be discerned in the long struggle by man toward release from the torments of poverty, insecurity, and deprivation, and, to make this release possible, toward a strongly interventionist, humanitarian, and policy-setting political state.[12]

In Europe the tendency was represented by J. A. Hobson and L. T. Hobhouse. In America it was represented by the Progressive movement that elected two of its leaders president in the early twentieth century. In this country, as Nisbet wrote, "both Theodore Roosevelt and Woodrow Wilson made the Presidency a 'bully pulpit' for the gospel of progress through political intervention."[13]

One of the problems with the doctrine of progress as it has influenced American political science is that it is bound up with pessimism about the possibility of knowledge. Robert Nisbet has identified a tension between that pessimism and the traditional idea of progress that has animated the West: "Of all challenges to which the idea of progress is subjected in our time, none is more deadly in possibility than the present fast-changing position of knowledge and of the man of knowledge."[14]

The early works of the new American political science helped to effect that intellectual revolution described in 1925 by Charles E. Merriam:

> [T]he changing intellectual structure of the time suggests significant advances in the form and content of political inquiry. . . . It is clear that the importance of the role of philosophy and religion in shaping men's minds politically has declined during the last generation. . . . Speculative philosophy took control of politics during the seventeenth and eighteenth centuries and held its grip until the eighteenth . . . [P]hilosophers of the significance of Locke, Hobbes, Hegel no longer are able to impose their classifications and categories upon the human mind in the field of government. . . . [T]hey are apparently less adequate to meet the problems of the modern world.[15]

Merriam's avowed purpose in tracing this revolution in political thought shows the extent to which the founders were successful in replacing philosophy with history:

> We are in fact coming into a new world, with new social conditions and with new modes of thought and inquiry, and we may well inquire what direction and form our politics must take if it is to interpret and express these new tendencies of the new world.[16]

Merriam divided the history of political study into four phases: *a priori* and deductive, until 1850; historical and comparative, 1850-1900; observation, survey and measurement, beginning in 1900; psychological, beginning about 1925.[17]

The status of political philosophy in the new American political science is perhaps best illustrated by passages from Westel W. Willoughby's *An Examination of the Nature of the State: A Study in Political Philosophy*. At the outset, Willoughby indicates that political philosophy is but one of four fields in political science. The four fields are:

> First, Descriptive Political Science, dealing with a description of the various forms of political organization; secondly, Historical Political Science, dealing with the inquiry as to the manner and order in which political forms or governments have appeared and developed; thirdly, the Art of Government, or "politics" properly so called, dealing with the principles that should control the administration of public affairs; finally, Political Theory or Philosophy, concerned with the philosophi-

cal examination of the various concepts upon which the whole science of politics rests.[18]

The field of political philosophy is further subdivided into general political theory, particular political theory, and the history of political theories. Political philosophy is in no sense superior, or even prior, to the other fields of political science.

Moreover, political philosophy, as Willoughby conceived of it, was a very narrow and specialized field of inquiry. Willoughby excluded Aristotle, Machiavelli, and Montesquieu from the ranks of political philosophers because they were concerned with the science of politics rather than contributing to the development of the idea of the State. In fact, Willoughby uses the term "political philosophy" as a translation of the German term (*allgemeine Staatslehre*) usually translated "general State theory." But State theory is not identical with political philosophy, it is what is left when the most important questions of political philosophy are assumed to be answered by history.

The starting point of Willoughby's treatise is a series of definitions, including the definitions of "state," "nation," and "government." The definitions presuppose that the reader is familiar with states, nations, and governments, and yet the definitions are not drawn from common discourse about political phenomena but from the treatises of German and French writers. The most curious point to be drawn from Willoughby's chapter of definitions is that, because "Government is purely mechanical and governed by no general laws," the study of "Government lies wholly without the field of Political Theory, and is comprehended within the domains of descriptive and historical politics."[19]

Willoughby is, then, in an awkward position. At the outset, he distinguishes between the "State" and the "government." All of the "machinery" by which public purposes are formulated and executed is assigned the name "government" and dismissed from the concern of political philosophy. "Thus, as we shall see," he wrote, "the term 'State' is, when strictly considered, an abstract term."[20] The task Willoughby set for himself, therefore, was to examine the nature of an abstract term.

He undertook that task, in the first instance, by seeking out the origin of the State. This is a historical inquiry, although an abstract one: Willoughby did not trace the development of particular States, but attempted to isolate the common element in the history of all States. The origin of the State, he concluded was in a phenomenon of group psychology.

> [I]n the State, in the body politic, we have a unity created out of a mere sum of individuals by means of a sentiment of community of feeling and mutuality of interest, and this sentiment finds expression in the creation of a political power, and the subjection of the community to its authority. . . . [T]his essential psychological element must first exist subjectively in the minds of the people, and then become objective in laws and political institutions.[21]

But the State is not identical with that psychological phenomenon. The State exists only when the psychological unity is given outward form in governmental machinery.

It thus frequently happens that there exists in the minds of a community of people a desire for a political unity of a particular sort, and that this desire is of sufficient strength to maintain the unity of a State, were it once established and organized, but that objective conditions prevent for many years the realization of such an end.[22] So the State cannot have potential, but only actual, existence. The State is the product not of the consent of the individuals it comprises but of a feeling of national unity expressed only in the foundation of the State itself. The only test of the legitimacy of the State would seem to be existence: if it exists it is legitimate.

Not only does the State gain legitimacy by merely existing, but its every act becomes authoritative. Every rule or decision of the State is law, and nothing else is law; the law is unqualifiedly binding upon every subject. Willoughby adds that "it follows as a logical deduction, that, since no one can be bound by one's own will, the sovereign political power must necessarily be incapable of legal limitation."[23] That "sovereign political power" Willoughby understands as "the highest power of the State without reference to the manner in which this power is exercised or in whose hands it rests."[24]

To be sure, the absolute power of the State is not equivalent to an absolutely powerful government. The State, as Willoughby understands it, is logically and chronologically prior to the government; the State constitutes the government and may limit it. The sovereign power, however, the absolute, unlimited power of the State, may be exercised by the whole people or by any part of the people, and that sovereign power can vest any or all of the State power in the government. Neither the identity of the sovereign nor the extent of the government's powers is within the concern of political philosophy, so called by Willoughby.

The limits of political philosophy, as Willoughby understands it, follow from the fact that the State, the politically organized people, is taken as the datum of political philosophy and sovereignty is defined as the legally unlimited power of the State. The question of who is to exercise the sovereign power and how they are to exercise it would seem to reopen the traditional question of political philosophy: "What is the best regime?" But Willoughby abjured such questions:

> The position taken in this treatise is that those persons or bodies are the sovereigns who have the legal power of expressing the will of the State. Behind these persons we do not as publicists or itirists need to look. . . . We leave to the sociologist or practical politician the examination of the nature and force of Public Opinion.[25]

Political philosophy was not distinguished from the study of public law; questions outside of public law Willoughby willingly left to historically based social science (sociology) or to the realm of practice. Political philosophy goes no farther than to

> seek for the location of the sovereign power in the body politic, [it is] concerned with the State as it then is and as actually organized. In pursuit, therefore, of this aim we have only to find that organ or those organs that may express the State's will. The problem does not involve the question of the ultimate source whence has been obtained by these organs the volitional power that they exercise.[26]

The, source of the sovereign power was to be found only by historical inquiry in the case of particular States.

As are the questions of who should rule and how they should rule, the question of the ends of rule are outside the scope of Willoughby's political philosophy. The aims of the State are whatever aims the State pursues. The State can choose among a number of possible ends, may indeed be its own end.[27] The ends of particular States are to be determined only from the history of those States. The legitimate ends of the state, in general, are dictated by a historical process which is as yet incomplete. "In a multitude of directions the force of conditions will cause the State to become increasingly important not only as a conservative but as a constructive agent."[28] Willoughby ventured predictions, but not prescriptions; for example: "the greatest extension of the State's powers will probably be seen in the ultimate ownership and operation . . . of all those industries termed 'natural monopolies.'"[29]

But not all historical trends point toward greater State power:

> It is to be recognized, however, that together with these forces that tend
> to encourage and increase the activities of the State are others that will
> render less necessary a resort to this power. . . . With increasing civili-
> zation will come higher morality, broadened altruism, and widened
> intellectual horizon. These are the forces which may be depended upon
> for the correction of imperfect conditions as they arise, without the in-
> tervention of the State.[30]

There are, therefore, no permanent "ends" or "aims" of the State.
Conditions arise, and are more or less imperfect; forces are at work
which render the intervention of the State more or less advantageous.
The sovereign power in a particular State determines what ends or aims
that State will pursue at any given time in the State's history.

Willoughby's "political philosophy" repeatedly defers to history and
practice, whence come the answers to the questions about politics that
have hitherto been regarded by political philosophers as most important.
In the concluding chapter of his treatise, Willoughby made clear that he
regarded political philosophy itself as a historical discipline.

> An intimate relation has ever existed between abstract political theo-
> ries, and the particular objective conditions which have given rise to
> them, and which they have been called upon to explain. . . . [Such theo-
> ries have] ever been intimately associated with, and limited by, particu-
> lar conditions of fact. . . . [A]ny system that we may evolve, will prove
> inadequate when called upon in the future to explain political condi-
> tions, the character of which our limited powers of prevision render it
> impossible for us to foresee.[31]

Because political philosophy is a historical discipline, Willoughby
devotes a section of his treatise to "The Development of the Abstract
Idea of the State."[32] The section traces the development of State theory
along with the development of the modern national State: an unbroken
record of progressively more complete understanding.

Woodrow Wilson treated the State exclusively in historical terms.
His treatise, *The State: Elements of Historical and Practical Politics*,[33]
bears the sub-subtitle: *A Sketch of Institutional History and Administration*. Institutional history provided Wilson with the answers to questions
that political philosophers wrestled with:

This, then, is the sum of the whole matter: the end of government is the facilitation of the objects of society. The rule of governmental action is necessary cooperation; the method of political development is conservative adaptation, shaping old habits into nil ones, modifying old means to accomplish new ends.[34]

In Wilson's analysis, the ends of government were to be discerned from what governments actually did. He began his treatment of the question, "What are the functions of government?" by discoursing on the "nature" of the question. That discourse was an assertion of what later came to be called the "fact-value" distinction:

It is important to notice at the outset a single general point touching the nature of this question. It is in one aspect obviously a simple *question of fact*; and yet there is another phase of it, in which it becomes as evidently a question of opinion.[35]

The distinction is important because over and over again the question of fact has been confounded with that widely different question, "What ought the functions of government to be?" The two questions should be kept entirely separate in treatment.[36]

Wilson proposed to answer the fact question merely by discovering what functions existing governments actually performed: "When asked, therefore, What are the functions of government? we must ask in return, Of what government? Different states have different conceptions of their duty, and so undertake different things."[37]

However, the different States did not come to have different conceptions of their duty through some process of collective ratiocination. Duty and function, like everything else, are the products of history and circumstance. The different States "have had their own peculiar origins, their own characteristic histories; circumstance has moulded them; necessity, interest, or caprice has variously guided them."[38] It is that one searches in vain for a theoretical discussion of the functions of the State or of government in Wilson's writings as a political scientist. The question can be answered only in terms of the peculiar history and circumstance of particular States.

Henry Jones Ford, whom Wilson recruited to be professor of American government at Princeton, went so far as to produce a *Natural History of the State*.[39] In that work, Ford examined the state from the point of view of a number of historical sciences, including biology, psychology, linguistics, anthropology, and genetics. His findings he reported in the last chapter of the book, entitled "First Principles in Politics." Some of those conclusions are: "Man is the product of Social Evolution."[40] "The State is the permanent and universal frame of human existence . . . and it antedates the differentiation of Man from the antecedent animal stock."[41] "Man did not make the State; the State made Man. . . . The State is absolute and unconditioned in relation to [the Individual]."[42] "Sovereignty is the supremacy of the State over all its parts. It has degrees, proportioned to the development of governmental structure, being greatest in advanced forms of the State."[43]

Ford offered these conclusions from the Darwinian hypothesis as a way of resolving the "contrariety of opinion" found in "political specula-tion."[44] Ford's "natural history" is but a further refinement of Wil-loughby's and Wilson's resort to political history to resolve the same problem. Speculative theory, in the view of such founders of the new political science as Willoughby, Wilson, and Ford, led only to differ-ences of opinion about the political things. History (or natural history) seemed to offer unambiguous answers.

The most common starting point for the argument in favor of replacing political philosophy with history as the basis of political science is just that argument that the history of political thought is the history of differences opinion, each opinion refuting the rest. "Actually, however," the assumption is false, because "that history does not teach us that the political philosophies of the past refute each other. It teaches us merely that they contradict each other."[45]

NOTES

1. Leo Strauss, "What Is Political Philosophy?" in *What Is Political Philosophy? and Other Studies* (New York: Free Press, 1959), 15.
2. Leo Strauss, "Political Philosophy and History" in *What Is Political Philosophy?*, 59.
3. Walter J. Shepard, "Political Science," in *The History and Prospects of the Social Sciences*, ed. by Harry E. Barnes (New York: Alfred A. Knopf, 1925), 425.
4. Strauss, "Political Philosophy and History," 59.
5. Raymond G. Gettell, *Problems in Political Evolution* (Boston: Ginn and Company, 1914), 10–11.
6. Gettell, *Problems in Political Evolution*, 3–4.
7. Gettell, *Problems in Political Evolution*, 14.
8. Gettell, *Problems in Political Evolution*, 9.
9. Gettell, *Problems in Political Evolution*, 25.

10. Robert Nisbet, *The History of the Idea of Progress* (New York: Basic Books, 1980), 277.

11. Nisbet, *History of the Idea*, 304–305.

12. Nisbett, *History of the Idea*, 304.

13. Nisbett, *History of the Idea*, 304.

14. Nisbett, *History of the Idea*, 340.

15. Charles E. Merriam, *New Aspects of Politics* (Chicago: The University of Chicago Press, 1925), 6–7.

16 Merriam, *New Aspects*, 2.

17. Merriam, *New Aspects*, 49.

18. Westel Woodbury Willoughby, *An Examination of the Nature of the State* (Farmingdale, N.Y.: Dabor Social Science Publications, 1978), 4–5. [This edition is a photographic reproduction of the first edition, published by Macmillan and Co., 1896.]

19. Willoughby, *An Examination*, 8. The capital G is in each instance Willoughby's.

20. Willoughby, *An Examination*, 8.

21. Willoughby, *An Examination*, 119.

22. Willoughby, *An Examination*, 120.

23. Willoughby, *An Examination*, 182.

24. Willoughby, *An Examination*, 183.

25. Willoughby, *An Examination*, 293–294.

26. Willoughby, *An Examination*, 305.

27. Willoughby, *An Examination*, 315.

28. Willoughby, *An Examination*, 341.

29. Willoughby, *An Examination*, 348.

30. Willoughby, *An Examination*, 349–350.

31. Willoughby, *An Examination*, 380–381.

32. Willoughby, *An Examination*, 385–396.

33. Woodrow Wilson, *The State: Elements of Historical and Practical Politics* (Boston: D.C. Heath & Co., 1897). [Originally published in 1889.]

34 Wilson, *The State*, 668.

35. Wilson, *The State*, 637.

36. Wilson, *The State*, 637–638.

37. Wilson, *The State*, 637.

38. Wilson, *The State*, 637.

39. Henry Jones Ford, *The Natural History of the State: An Introduction to Political Science* (Princeton, N.J.: Princeton University Press, 1915).

40. Ford, *Natural History*, 174.

41. Ford, *Natural History*, 175.

42. Ford, *Natural History*, 175–176.

43. Ford, *Natural History*, 175–176.

44. Ford, 1–9 *Natural History*, and *passim*.

45. Strauss, "Political Philosophy and History," 62.

Chapter Five

DECLARATION OF INDEPENDENCE

The United States of America is the first nation in the history of the world to be founded on a philosophical principle of universal applicability. That principle is the principle of equality: "We hold these truths to be self-evident: that all men are created equal."

The Declaration of Independence is both an assertion of a particular understanding of the nature of man and of the political things and also the founding document of the American Republic. As such, it stands at the intersection of political philosophy and political action. It is the central document of the tradition of American political science as that political science was understood prior to the professionalization and academization of the discipline. Rejection of the Declaration of Independence, of its teachings, and of its applicability to our own times, was a necessary part of the foundation of a new American political science.

To say as much is neither a naked assertion nor a bold act of interpretation. The founders of the new political science recognized the necessity of freeing American politics from the eighteenth-century conceptions embodied in the Declaration. Hence, Westel W. Willoughby declared (quoting approvingly from sociologist Lester F. Ward):

[O]ur Declaration of Independence, which recites that Government derives its just powers from the consent of the governed has already been outgrown. It is no longer the consent, but the positively known will of the governed, from which the government now derives its powers.[1]

And John W. Burgess assessed the significance of the Declaration in this way:

A nation and a state did not spring into existence through that declaration, as dramatic publicists are wont to express it. . . . The significance of the proclamation was this: a people testified thereby the consciousness of the fact that they had become, in the progressive development of history, one whole, separate, and adult nation, and a national state.[2]

Moreover, the rejection was recognized by the first historian of the new, professional discipline, Charles E. Merriam, who wrote in 1920 that recent political theory in the United States "shows a decided tendency away from many doctrines that were held by the men of 1776. . . . The Revolutionary doctrines of an original state of nature, natural rights, the social contract, the idea that the function of the government is limited to the protection of person and property,—none of these finds wide acceptance among the leaders in the development of political science. . . . [T]he rejection of these doctrines is a scientific tendency rather than a popular movement."[3]

The rejection of the Declaration of Independence took two forms, the one explicit, and the other implicit.

The explicit form is found in the writing of Burgess, Willoughby, Wilson, and others, who dismissed the natural rights thesis and the doctrine of social contract out of hand, and who described the Declaration, if they bothered with it at all, as a tract for its times, a rhetorical incident of the Revolution. The implicit rejection of the Declaration is found in the works of such Progressives as J. Allen Smith and Charles A. Beard, who appropriated the Declaration as a statement of general democratic and revolutionary principles, but who openly or covertly denied the propositions asserted in the Declaration to be self-evident truths.

The philosophical principle of the Declaration is the principle of human equality. But that is not enough; the principle of equality implies the state of nature and natural rights. The best statement of that implication is:

> The idea of the equality of all men, within the eighteenth century horizon, was connected with the idea of a state of nature, a pre-political state in which there was no government, no lawful subordination of one man to another man. . . . The concept of a state of nature, as a pre-political state, highly undesirable, yet tolerable, is among the axiomatic premises of the Declaration of Independence.[4]

The doctrine of the Declaration is the basis of the traditional American political science; and the concept of a state of nature is an axiomatic premise of that doctrine. How was the doctrine of the state of nature treated in the works of the founders of the new academic political science?

John W. Burgess "had nothing but contempt for the elegant balances of eighteenth-century political theory, especially the fiction of Locke's notion of contract."[5] Rather, he "followed the current political theory in repudiating the doctrines of natural law and the social contract, declaring that they were wholly contrary to our knowledge of the historical development of political institutions."[6]

An indication of the significance Woodrow Wilson attached to the Declaration is that in his five-volume history of the United States he disposes of the Declaration in just two sentences:

> But by midsummer it was deemed best to make a formal Declaration of Independence. North Carolina was the first to instruct her delegates to take that final and irrevocable step; but most of the other colonies were ready to follow her lead; and on July 4th Congress adopted the impressive Declaration which Mr. Jefferson had drawn up in the name of its committee.[7]

Wilson earned his initial academic reputation with his doctoral dissertation, published as *Congressional Government*. But the early book on which he worked hardest and longest was his political science treatise, *The State*, "an historical and comparative study of various types of government."[8] The book was a textbook suitable for general courses in political science, in which the largest part was devoted to comparative government. Wilson was not reluctant to put forward his version of *allgemeine Staatslehre* in his book, and "[t]hroughout its chapters run a philosophy of law and government, subordinated, however, to the study of the structure and spirit of the political institutions described."[9]

In *The State*, Wilson dismissed the notion that political theory could explain the legitimacy of political power or the obligation of subjects to obey the law. He concentrated instead on the evolution of known States. He was particularly hostile to the natural rights-social contract theory, and it is with that theory that he begins his section on "theories concerning the origin of the state":

> The most famous, and for our present purposes most important, of these theories is that which ascribes the origin of government to a "social compact" among primitive men. . . . This theory always begins with the assumption that there exists, outside of and above the laws of men, a Law of Nature. . . . All its chief commentators considered it the abstract standard to which human law should conform.[10]

But the origin of government in the contract of men originally under the laws of nature has been refuted, not by logic, but by anthropology. "Modern research into the early history of mankind," Wilson wrote, has "revealed facts which render it impossible for us to accept any of these views."[11] The contract theory "simply has no historical foundation" because in actual States, government was based originally on status and kinship.[12] The theory, according to Wilson, was at odds with the facts.

Willoughby, too, produced as his first major work a treatise on the nature of the State, and like Burgess's and Wilson's it followed the tradition of *allegemeine Staatslehre*, the Germanic "general State theory." Willoughby, too, began by rejecting those political theories that relied on external standards for judging political action. Every species of natural law or natural rights theory was treated with scorn. Willoughby recognized that the natural rights-social contract theory was the basis of American politics,[13] but he did not acknowledge that in attacking the theory of the Declaration of Independence, or Jefferson, or the Founding Fathers, he might be at all changing the authority of American politics. He in fact repeatedly used the words of the Declaration when describing the political theory under attack.

The "logical ground" upon which all social contract theories rest is postulation of "a pre-civic, non-political condition" in which there are "no rules regulative of human conduct, save those afforded by the so-called 'Laws of Nature.'"[14] The "Laws of Nature" are, of course, the rules of conduct on which the Founding Fathers based their appeal in the Declaration. Moreover, Willoughby recognized that the "Laws of Nature" underlay the traditional "doctrines of constitutional government and popular sovereignty."[15]

When, however, we come to consider the history of the theories of Constitutional Government and Popular Sovereignty, we shall find that long after the Contract Theory had been generally discredited and discarded, the theory of Natural Law maintained its influence in the form of so-called "natural," "inalienable," "imprescriptible" rights of man. In fact, in this guise, it is still widely held at the present day.[16]

Once again, Willoughby used the words of the Declaration to describe the theory under attack: "inalienable rights."

But Willoughby could not accept that "logical ground," and, in fact, rejected both the practical and the moral authority of natural laws:

> [W]e have to demonstrate that, when in a "State of Nature" men are said to be ruled by "Laws of Nature," these laws cannot be held to be even of a moral validity. . . . In such a "State of Nature," there is, if not *ex hypothesi*, logically, at least, an utter and entire absence of human association and concert of action, the only rules for the regulation of conduct that can possibly obtain [are] the natural instincts of all living beings, men and brutes alike, to maintain their own existences.[17]

The political philosophy of natural rights and social contract, authoritative because of the "laws of Nature and of nature's God," justified the existence of government on the ground that the existence of government made men secure in the enjoyment of what was theirs by nature. For Willoughby, that was nonsense: "The State is thus justified by its manifest potency as an agent for the progress of mankind."[18]

The second principal teaching of the Declaration of Independence is that government is legitimately established only for limited purposes, namely to "secure these rights" with which men are naturally endowed. The powers of government, if they are just, are derived "from the consent of the governed," and if the existence of government becomes "destructive" of the rights for the security of which it was called into being, "it is the right of the people to alter or abolish it." Since the end of government is defined by the "laws of Nature and of nature's God," it is always and everywhere the same.

Wilson did acknowledge that "there are natural and imperative limits to state action."[19] Those limits are the limits of necessity: the objects of government are those for which action on the part of society as a whole is necessary and not merely convenient. This stance Wilson took in opposition to socialist opinions about what government ought to do. Wilson had distinguished the "objects of government" from the "functions of government," the former being matters of opinion, the latter matters of fact to be ascertained by the historical and comparative method.[20]

But the limit is no longer merely Wilson's opinion:

> Unless the state has a nature which is quite clearly defined by that invariable, universal, immutable mutual interdependence which runs beyond the family relations and cannot be satisfied by family ties, we have absolutely no criterion by which we can limit, except arbitrarily, the activities of the state.[21]

This "nature" seems to have to be willed and asserted; it is a "nature" to be imposed by men on the state that has developed historically.

Nature, moreover, might limit opinion, but not fact. The question of fact is resolved by determining which are the "functions which, in one shape or another, all governments alike have undertaken."[22] A partial list of the functions of government includes: regulation of trade, industry, and labor; maintenance of roads, railways, and postal and telegraph systems; distribution of gas and water; sanitation; education; conservation; care of the poor and incapable; and enforcement of sumptuary laws.[23] History has thus given to government a body of functions quite as comprehensive as any socialist could wish.

Willoughby, too, rejected any conception according to which the end of government (or the aims of the State) would be fixed:

> The aims of the State in general are the functions for the performance of which the State is essentially and peculiarly adapted, and the aims which, according to our conception of the highest good of humanity, it seems desirable should be obtained. . . . [T]his conception is one that must necessarily be based upon the study of present and past social conditions and tendencies. Therefore, just as our view differs from those views that have been held in former periods of history. . . . so too, in the years to come, such may be the nature of developed conditions of life . . . that our conception of what is either desirable or attainable will be so altered that the ideal aim of the State will be otherwise formulated.[24]

The end of government is thus not always and everywhere the same, but varies according to the "conception of the highest good of humanity" which is dominant at any particular time.

Willoughby relegated the teaching of the Declaration of Independence to the "individualistic" conception, which he rejected in favor of the "common welfare" conception of the good of humanity. "According to the individualistic school, the importance of the so-called private rights of property, life and liberty is greatly emphasized, and the proper province of the State held to be limited solely to the protection of them."[25]

The "individualistic camp," while clearly inclusive of the Founding Fathers, is typified in Willoughby's book by Herbert Spencer, Paul Janet, and, most importantly, Wilhelm von Humboldt. To the extent that Willoughby is willing to acknowledge the legitimacy of such a viewpoint at all, it is only insofar as it is justified on utilitarian grounds. "We are of course not concerned here with alleged support given to this view by the doctrine of Natural Rights. The insufficiency of that doctrine we have already shown."[26]

Willoughby spent much ink disposing of the utilitarian justification for limited governmental ends. Then, having effected "the refutation of the individualistic doctrines," he proceeded to assert that the State may exercise all those powers necessary for those "functions we term 'non-essential' or 'common welfare' functions." In that category he included "the economic, industrial and moral interests of the people," assumed "because their public administration is supposed to be advantageous to the people."[27]

Which of those functions are to be undertaken, and when, and under what circumstances, were not, according to Willoughby, to be predetermined.

> The determination of just what powers shall be assumed by the State, is solely one of expediency, and as such lies within the field of Politics, or the Art of Government, and not within the domain of political theory. . . In each instance the particular circumstances of the case must determine whether or not the advantages to be derived from the public control in a particular case are more than offset by the weakening of the self-reliance of the people . . . This is practically, the rule followed by all modern civilized States.[28]

Willoughby then went on to discuss the "trends" in assumptions of State power. He was reassured in this by the continuous progress being made in political and administrative science—in the past, the "administrations of public affairs was largely dominated by individual and class selfishness," leading to a presumption against State action; but "[a]s this disturbing factor is removed by the widening of political rights and the perfection of political machinery, this prejudice will be removed."[29] Since the only difference between Willoughby's "general welfare" school and socialism was the latter's "greater confidence felt in the efficiency and advisability of State action, and hence a greater willingness to use it,"[30] the tendency of history as a guide to the role of government was in the direction of ever greater government control.

Therefore,

> [i]t is not necessary to recite here the numerous and important instances during comparatively recent years in which the State has widened her boundaries under the impelling influence of the causes we have enumerated. If one were asked to characterize in a single sentence the development of government during the present (i.e., nineteenth] century, it could not be better done than by describing such development as one wherein the purely political duties of the State have become progressively less important as compared with its other functions.[31]

The determinant of legitimacy of governmental power is thus "development," which is to say, "history." Willoughby's "study in political philosophy" is reduced to a study of the direction of historical development.

Others of the early generation of American academic political scientists, especially those who studied at Columbia or Johns Hopkins, took the same line as Burgess, Wilson, and Willoughby. Frank J. Goodnow, for example, the Burgess protégé who became first president of the A.P.S.A., also "repudiated the doctrine of natural rights and the social contract as the basis of organized political society, relying rather upon historical and evolutionary considerations and tendencies."[32] And Henry Jones Ford, whom Wilson added to the faculty at Princeton, included among the conclusions of his *Natural History of the State*: "Rights are not innate but are derivative. They exist in the State but not apart from the State."

Raymond G. Gettell took a similar tack in his *Problems in Political Evolution*.[33] The idea of natural rights had to be considered as a product of the eighteenth century, a temporary and unsuccessful attempt to reconcile concepts of liberty and authority:

> In the eighteenth century men spoke much of natural rights. Life, liberty, property, the pursuit of happiness, and other similar privileges were considered inalienable rights under the laws of nature. . . . Analy-

sis shows the fallacy in such thinking. In a state of nature liberty would be impossible. Each person would have rights only as he could secure them by force.[34]

The theory was part of a "reaction, against the paternalism of the despotic monarchies of the eighteenth century."[35]

Gettell posited a general evolutionary development, which, though uneven, must be characterized as progress:

> In contrast to those theories of state origin which arose as subjective deductions when man's thinking was uncritical and unhistorical, or which were deliberately formulated to support the authority of certain privileged classes, or which overemphasized certain factors to the neglect of others, the modern theory of state origin tries to ascertain the actual facts of human progress . . . and to realize that the rise of political institutions is not a separate process, but a phase of the general development of man and society.[36]

But "[t]his progress has taken different forms and has proceeded with varying rapidity among different peoples."[37] Therefore, contrary to the principles of the Declaration of Independence, wherein it is asserted that governments are instituted among men to secure the enjoyment of natural rights, "the end to which a state, at any given time, should chiefly direct its efforts depends, of course, upon the point that has been reached in its development."[38] The result of the evolutionary process is the modern state, i.e., the democratic nation-state, and

> [T]he purpose of the modern state, accordingly, includes a more or less composite aim at securing order and justice for its citizens, providing for its own continued and developing existence, and promoting the progress of the world at large.[39]

J. Allen Smith represented a distinct school within the American political science of the period. Having earned his Ph.D. at the University of Michigan, he ultimately became professor of political science in the University of Washington. He had been exposed to the Germanic historicism of the founders of American political science, but was much more influenced by the political reformism of the Progressive movement. In his published writings he adopted a kind of crude economic determinism.

Smith's treatment of the Declaration of Independence is worth noting separately because it is not, at first sight, the same kind of out-of-hand rejection that the Declaration met with from Burgess, Wilson, and Willoughby. Smith rather smothered the Declaration by holding it too close to his breast. For him it was the symbol and expression of vital, revolutionary democracy, the product of the most democratic of times:

> No sooner, however, had the controversy reached the acute revolutionary stage, than the forces which had been silently and unconsciously working toward democracy, found an opportunity for political expression. . . . The people were ready for a larger measure of political democracy than the English Constitution of the eighteenth century permitted. To this new and popular view of government the Declaration of Independence gave expression. It contained an emphatic, formal and solemn disavowal of the political theory embodied in the English Constitution; affirmed that "all men are created equal"; that governments derive "their just powers from the consent of the governed"; and declared the right of the people to alter or to abolish the form of government.[40]

The authority to which the Declaration had appealed, the laws of Nature and of nature's God, universally available to men through reason, was no authority for Smith. The "theory of government expressed in the Declaration of Independence," of which the Constitution was made out to be a repudiation,[41] amounted to no more than "its express and implied advocacy of democracy."[42]

Smith professed an attachment to the "political views expressed in the Declaration of Independence,"[43] but presented those views as unalloyed, unqualified, unlimited, direct rule of the majority on all questions. But that is quite far from the actual political teaching of the Declaration: that all men, by nature, enjoy equality of right, and on account of that equality are entitled to enjoy the rights of life, liberty, and the pursuit of happiness; that they cannot divest themselves of those rights, but may establish government for the protection of those natural rights; and that government so established is legitimate only if formed by their own consent for the purpose of protecting men's natural rights.

Writing in 1922, a few years after the period treated in the instant work, Carl L. Becker surveyed the attitudes of various nineteenth-century intellectuals toward the philosophy of the Declaration of Independence.[44] Becker identified the German historical school, broadly defined to include the followers of both Leopold von Ranke and Hegel, as the chief source of hostility to the natural rights theory of the Declaration in the latter part of the nineteenth century. "For half a century this philosophy was the chief intellectual weapon for combating the natural rights doctrine of the eighteenth century, the chief intellectual bulwark" against the egalitarian tendencies of the French Revolution.[45] But Becker also reported the historicist critique of the Declaration from the point of view of Darwinian natural science:

> When so much of the universe showed itself amenable to the reign of a purely material natural law, it was difficult to suppose that man (a creature in many respects astonishingly like the higher forms of apes) could have been permitted to live under a special dispensation. It was much simpler to assume one origin for all life and one law for all growth.[46]

Science itself was "steadily dissolving its own 'universal and eternal laws' into a multiplicity of incomplete and temporary hypotheses."[47]

For all that, however, Becker himself read the Declaration rather as Smith did, that is as in some vague way giving comfort to democracy and humanity. Becker's Declaration was founded "upon a naive faith in the instinctive virtues of humankind," and embodied "a humane and engaging faith" that "invited men to promote in themselves the humanity which bound them to their fellows."[48] It seemed to Becker that to "ask whether the natural rights philosophy of the Declaration of Independence is true or false is essentially a meaningless question"; rather, it is to be tested pragmatically: it is "true"—the quotation marks are Becker's—if it "enables [those who believe it] to think of themselves as having chosen the nobler part."[49] To one who reads Smith and Becker the question must occur whether the Declaration is not in safer hands when it is attacked by its true enemies than when it is embraced by some of its supposed friends.

NOTES

1. Westel W. Willoughby, *An Examination of the Nature of the State: A Study in Political Philosophy* (Farmingdale, N.Y.: Dabor Social Science Publications, 1978), 141. [This is a photographic reprint of the original edition published by Macmillan and Co., 1896.]

2. John W. Burgess, *Political Science and Comparative Constitutional Law* (Boston: Ginn & Company, 1890), vol. 1, 100.

3. Charles E. Merriam, *A History of American Political Theories* (New York: The Macmillan Company, 1920), 332.

4. Harry V. Jaffa, *Crisis of the House Divided* (New York: Doubleday & Co., Inc., 1959), 318.

5. Michael H. Frisch, "Urban Theorists, Urban Reform, and American Political Culture in the Progressive Period," *Political Science Quarterly* 97, no. 2 (Summer 1982): 299.

6. Charles E. Merriam, *American Political Ideas* (New York: The Macmillan Company, 1920), 379.

7. Woodrow Wilson, *A History of the American People* (New York: Harper & Brothers, 1902), vol. 2, 242.

8. Merriam, *American Political Ideas*, 382.

9. Merriam, *American Political Ideas*, 382.

10. Woodrow Wilson, *The State: Elements of Historical and Practical Politics* (Boston: D.C. Heath & Co., 1897), 11. [Originally published in 1889.]

11. Wilson, *The State*, 13.

12. Wilson, *The State*, 13–14.

13. Willoughby, *Nature of the State*, 87.

14. Willoughby, *Nature of the State*, 89.

15. Willoughby, *Nature of the State*, 91.

16. Willoughby, *Nature of the State*, 102.

17. Willoughby, *Nature of the State*, 106–107.

18. Willoughby, *Nature of the State*, 112.

19. Wilson, *The State*, 664.

20. Wilson, *The State*, 637–638.

21. Wilson, *The State*, 665–666.

22. Wilson, *The State*, 640.

23. Wilson, *The State*, 639–640.

24. Willoughby, *Nature of the State*, 309–310.

25. Willoughby, *Nature of the State*, 320.

26. Willoughby, *Nature of the State*, 325–326.

27. Willoughby, *Nature of the State*, 337–338.

28. Willoughby, *Nature of the State*, 338.

29. Willoughby, *Nature of the State*, 340.

30. Willoughby, *Nature of the State*, 339.

31. Willoughby, *Nature of the State*, 342.

32. Merriam, *American Political Ideas*, 390.

33. Raymond G. Gettell, *Problems in Political Evolution* (Boston: Ginn and Company, 1914).

34. Gettell, *Problems*, 201.

35. Gettell, *Problems*, 211.

36. Gettell, *Problems*, 79.

37. Gettell, *Problems*, 102.

38. Gettell, *Problems*, 360.

39. Gettell, *Problems*, 361.

40. J. Allen Smith, *The Spirit of American Government* (New York: The Macmillan Company, 1919), 13–14. [Originally published in 1907.]

41. Smith, *Spirit*, 218–219.

42. Smith, *Spirit*, 14.

43. Smith, *Spirit*, 14.

44. Carl L. Becker, *The Declaration of Independence: A Study in the History of Political Ideas* (New York: Vintage Books, 1942), 224–279. [Originally published in 1922.]

45. Becker, *Declaration*, 272.

46. Becker, *Declaration*, 274–275.

47. Becker, *Declaration*, 279.

48. Becker, *Declaration*, 278.

49. Becker, *Declaration*, 277.

Chapter Six

THE CONSTITUTION

Having attacked the principle of human equality and the idea of natural rights that flows from that principle, the new political science undertook to attack the political science underlying the Constitution of the United States. Like the attack on the Declaration of Independence, this was a manifestation of the general intellectual tendency of the movement: rejection of deduction and prescription in the name of induction, technique, and the idea of progress.

The Constitution itself was written as the frame of national government for the regime created in the Declaration of Independence. From the premises of the Declaration it follows that the Constitution derives its authority from the consent of the governed and from its being calculated to effect the future safety and happiness of the American people. Moreover, the government must have as its purpose for existence the preservation of the natural rights of the people who are to live under it. The experience of the founding generation of the Republic was of a government that had become destructive of those ends.

The political science of the Founders was calculated to make government strong enough to protect the citizen in the enjoyment of his life, liberty, and property, and yet not so strong as to become a threat to the citizen. Fortunately, the science of politics, like most sciences, had received vast improvement since the days of the ancient republics, and various principles had been discovered that tended to make such a government possible:

> The regular distribution of power into distinct departments; the intro-
> duction of legislative balances and checks; the institution of courts
> composed of judges holding their offices during good behavior; the
> representation of the people in the legislature by deputies of their own
> election . . . are means, and powerful means, by which the excellencies
> of republican government may be retained and its imperfections less-
> ened or avoided.[1]

To this catalog, of course, Publius (Hamilton) adds the device of federation to enlarge the orbit of the government. The political science of the Framers was aimed at breaking the violence of factional politics. By "faction," Publius understood

> a number of citizens, whether amounting to a majority or minority of
> the whole, who are united and actuated by some common impulse of
> passion, or of interest, adverse to the rights of other citizens, or to the
> permanent and aggregate interests of the community.[2]

For the Framers, it was the content of the opinion, and not merely the number of persons holding it that mattered. Their political science was intended to thwart factional rule even if the faction comprised a majority of the citizens. The Constitution envisions democratic government in which the majority accepts certain checks upon the exercise of its power: "A dependence on the people is, no doubt, the primary control of the government; but experience has taught mankind the necessity of auxil-iary precautions."[3]

It is perhaps an indication of the success of the old American political science that the founders of the new American political science did not perceive the problem of majority faction as a major threat to free government. The constitutional limits of majority rule, Publius (Madi-son)'s "auxiliary precautions," were perceived as limiting majority rule and, therefore, as curtailing democracy.

The vanguard of the attack on the Constitution was led by J. Allen Smith and Charles A. Beard. The former asserted[4] and the latter affected to demonstrate[5] that the Constitution was written with the object of protecting the economic interests of a particular class. According to Smith and Beard, the Constitution was framed for the purpose of frustrat-ing just such attempts at political reform and economic regulation as were frustrated on constitutional grounds during the early years of the Progressive Era.

The effect of their critique of the Constitution was described, in somewhat extravagant terms, by the liberal intellectual historian Vernon L. Parrington:

> With the flood of light thrown upon the fundamental law by the historians, the movement of liberalism passed quickly through successive phases of thought. After the first startled surprise it set about the necessary business of acquainting the American people with its findings in the confident belief that a democratic electorate would speedily democratize the instrument. Of this first stage the late Professor J. Allen Smith's *The Spirit of American Government* (1907) was the most adequate expression, a work that greatly influenced the program of the rising Progressive Party. But changes came swiftly and within half a dozen years the movement had passed from poltical programs to economic, concerned not so greatly with political democracy as with economic democracy. Of this second phase Professor Beard's *An Economic Interpretation of the Constitution* (1913) was the greatest intellectual achievement.[6]

Parrington attributed to Smith and Beard "the discovery that the drift toward plutocracy was not a drift away from the sprit of the Constitution, but an inevitable unfolding from its premises."[7]

Once it was accepted, first by intellectuals and later by the general public, that the characteristic features of American constitutionalism—federalism, bicameralism, separation of powers, checks and balances, indirect elections, staggered terms of office, and so on—are not the necessary principles of rule of law, but are rather devices to ensure the continued dominance of the rich over the regime, there is no longer any reason for democrats to feel bound by those features. With the barriers erected by class interest removed, the way was clear for a democratic political science.

But crude economic determinism was not the preferred mode of analysis in the new political science. The crucial defect of the Constitution, from the point of view of the politics of progress, was not economic, but chronological. It was simply impossible for eighteenth-century man to address the needs of twentieth-century man. (The same argument is familiar in our time in the vulgar form: "James Madison did not have the atomic bomb to worry about.")

One of the functions of the new political science, as its practitioners understood it, was to replace eighteenth-century superstition with twentieth-century knowledge about political things. The superior understanding available to the twentieth century would render unnecessary the precautions of the Founders. Despite the efforts of Smith, Beard, and their followers, it was not necessary to assume that the authors of the Constitution had other than the purest motives, for it was not their motives, but their science, which was ultimately to blame. Acceptance of the Smith-Beard critique would, seemingly, require restructuring of the American government to remove the class bias inherent in the Constitution. But the new political scientists offered an alternative: reform according to a scientific understanding of politics and administration.

Woodrow Wilson, writing in 1885, already understood that the attitude of the new political science represented a radical change in the self-understanding of the American regime:

> We are the first Americans to hear our own countrymen ask whether the Constitution is still adapted to serve the purposes for which it was intended; the first to entertain any serious doubts about the superiority of our own institutions as compared with the systems of Europe; the first to think of reorganizing the administrative machinery of the federal government.[8]

Indeed, the whole of Wilson's book answers the description just provided, and it ends with a ringing appeal to replace the "political witchcraft" of the Constitution with the "expedients necessary to make self-government among us a straightforward thing of simple method, single, unstinted power, and clear responsibility."[9] Wilson's reference to "political witchcraft" may seem a bit flippant, but it was meant to indicate the relationship that the prescientific politics of the Framers of the Constitution had to the political science of the Progressive Era. (In a similar vein, we are accustomed to hearing various species of economics denounced as "voodoo.")

The critique of the Constitution was by no means limited to the radicals and Progressives, but it permeated the whole of the new political science. John W. Burgess, for example, in suggesting that the amending process be simplified to make it more responsive to national majorities, wrote that "development is as much a law of state life as existence. Prohibit the former, and the latter is the existence of the body after the spirit has departed."[10] He declared himself in sympathy with those jurists and publicists (i.e., writers on public law) who were "beginning to feel, and rightly too, that present considerations, relations and requirements should be the chief consideration."[11]

Burgess, a conservative nationalist, objected mainly to federalism as a constitutional principle. Because he regarded the State as the nation organized politically and held that within the State there must be a single, absolute sovereign, Burgess regarded American federalism as anomalous. He resolutely abstained from using the word "state" unqualified as the name of the lesser political units in America (despite the style of the Union and the use of the word in the Constitution), referring always to "commonwealths." And he wrote:

> We have not yet by any means perfected our system. Our conceptions in reference to civil liberties are still clouded by crude notions about the federal system, and its requirements as to citizenship.[12]

Burgess regarded federal government as a transitional form appropriate for use by a State in the process of consolidation. However, he speculated that a government of centralized legislation and federal (or decentralized) administration might be "the form of the future, the ultimate, the ideal form, at least for all great states."[13]

Burgess's enthusiasm for a theoretically pure national State waned after the election of Woodrow Wilson to the presidency in 1912[14] and he thereafter adopted a more conventional outlook on the utility of federalism: "[i]n this distribution of governmental powers between two or more sets of governmental organs there is a certain security that the realm of Individual Immunity against governmental power will not be encroached upon."[15] Burgess's critique was always theoretical in the sense that the forms of the Constitution did not fit neatly into the scheme of analysis that Burgess believed embodied the general tendencies of universal history.

The younger generation of political scientists, caught up as they were in the Progressive movement, criticized the Constitution more directly as being outmoded by the progress of society and technology. The Constitution had been written by and for the people of a small, agricultural, predominantly rural, coastal republic. It was written by and for men whose transport depended upon the horse or the sailboat, who had no factories or railroads. Such men, innocent of technological progress, of urbanization and industrialization, could not have foreseen, let alone provided for, the men living under the conditions that would prevail at the beginning of the twentieth century.

Frank J. Goodnow, a protégé of Burgess's at Columbia and the first president of the American Political Science Association, opened his book, *Social Reform and the Constitution*[16] with the declaration:

> The tremendous changes in political and social conditions due to the adoption of improved means of transportation and to the establishment of the factory system have brought with them problems whose solution seems to be impossible under the principles of law which were regarded as both axiomatic and permanently enduring at the end of the eighteenth century.[17]

The obsolete eighteenth-century principles included the ideas of natural right and social compact, which in turn rested upon an idea that nature provides standards of right independent of the historical development of nations and states. But that idea has been outmoded by the recognition of the evolutionary principle in science and the observation that social problems have become increasingly complex, taking forms that were unimaginable by an agrarian people without modern forms of transportation, communication, and industry. Therefore:

> The question naturally [sic] arises before those who have no belief in a static political society or in permanent political principles of universal application, but who, on the contrary, are of the opinion that political organizations must be so framed and governmental powers so formulated as to be in accord as far as possible with the actual economic and social situation,—Is the kind of political system which we commonly believe our fathers established one which can with advantage be retained unchanged in the changed conditions which are seen to exist.[18]

Goodnow challenged the various auxiliary precautions of American constitutional government severally as incompatible with the exigencies of the modern era. As to separation of powers:

> The force of the principle as a rule of law is also being weakened. With the development of the more complex conditions characteristic of modern life, it has been felt imperitive [sic] to depart at any rate from the strict application of the principle.[19]

Goodnow referred here primarily to the creation of administrative offices and agencies that are vested with the legislative power to make ordinances with the force of law, or with the judicial power to decide individual cases applying statutes or ordinances, or with both.

Nothing so much characterizes Goodnow's political science as his rejection of the doctrine of separation of powers in favor of a separation of politics from administration. The great mistake of the Founding

Fathers was their acceptance of Montesquieu's teaching that executive, legislative, and judicial functions should be carried out be different officers or bodies in the government. But this mistake was one to which the Founders were impelled by the times in which they lived.

> At the time our early constitutions, including the national Constitution, were framed, this principle of the separation of powers with its corollary, the separation of authorities, was universally accepted in this country.[20]

Goodnow, however, believed the principle to be unworkable in practice.[21] "What had been a somewhat nebulous theory of political science [by incorporation into the Constitution] became a rigid legal doctrine," Goodnow wrote, and, "What had been a somewhat attractive political theory in its nebulous form became at once an unworkable and inapplicable rule of law."[22] The doctrine of separation of powers could be maintained only by ignoring the discovery of modern political science that

> [t]here are, then, in all governmental systems two primary or ultimate functions of government, viz., the expression of the will of the state and the execution of that will. There are also in all states separate organs, each of which is mainly busied with the discharge of one of these functions. These functions are respectively, Politics and Administration.[23]

American government, both national and state, was inefficient in that, by attempting to maintain the tripartite separation, it distributed political and administrative functions artificially among government authorities.

Goodnow's general position in *Social Reform and the Constitution* was optimistic with respect to judicial review. Although many, perhaps most, of the reforms Goodnow thought desirable or necessary ran counter to his understanding of the intention of the Framers of the Constitution, he believed that the judiciary, and especially the Supreme Court of the United States, would so interpret the Constitution as to find those reforms constitutional. Goodnow accepted what is now termed the "living Constitution," that is the Constitution understood as a malleable mass of general good intentions available to be shaped by the courts to provide authority for desired measures.

However, Goodnow was disappointed that the courts did not, as of 1911, understand the nation's predicament to be as grave as Goodnow did. "Up to the present time, however, it may not be said that even in the

Supreme Court existing economic conditions have always been accorded the influence which they should have."[24] The subsequent statement of what degree of influence ought to be accorded reveals much about Goodnow's view of the role of the judiciary under the Constitution: laws advancing social reform, he wrote, are declared by that body to be unconstitutional not because their enactment is thought undesirable or inexpedient but because they cannot be made to conform to a conception of the organization and powers of government which we have inherited front the eighteenth century.[25]

Goodnow seems in this passage to suggest that it is the province of the judiciary so to interpret the Constitution as to liberate it from its subservience to eighteenth-century political theory and to adapt it to evolving social and economic needs.

Both Goodnow's general critique and his suggestion concerning the role of judges are echoed in the writings of Charles E. Merriam:

> The state and federal constitutions signalized the development of a written document in which certain "natural rights" of men were declared and guaranteed, a plan of government outlined, and provision made in most cases for continuous change. . . . Given the constitutions there came the question of their progressive adaptation to changing conditions. But the logic of interpretation was not the logic of their origin. Born in the spirit of revolution, they were applied under the influence of *stare decisis*; prophetic in outlook, they were applied in terms of precedent.[26]

Assessing the competing political views of the early twentieth century, Merriam wrote:

> Goodnow's discussion of social reform and the constitution seemed to represent the general trend of political theory toward a readier adaptation of the fundamental law to changing social and economic conditions.[27]

Merriam himself, writing during the period he described in his later book, distinguished between the revolutionary period and the "reactionary movement" that produced the Constitution.[28] In this Merriam may be said to have anticipated J. Allen Smith, except that unlike Smith he found evidence of the revolutionary period's enthusiasm for democracy not in the Declaration of Independence (which he understood better than Smith), but in the state constitutions framed during the Revolution.

Those state constitutions had almost uniformly provided for legislative supremacy rather than for strict separation of powers with checks and balances.[29]

Woodrow Wilson, had he never become president, would nevertheless have been remembered as one of the founders of the new American political science and as one of the intellectual leaders of the Progressive movement. As a political scientist, Wilson specialized in the field of public administration, but worked generally in the area of American government. His two most noted books, *Congressional Government* and *Constitutional Government in the United States*,[30] both dealt with the institutional arrangements of American government. *Congressional Government* was written in 1883–1884[31] and published in 1885; after being accepted for publication it was also accepted as Wilson's doctoral dissertation at the Johns Hopkins University. *Constitutional Government* was written as a series of lectures to be given in 1907, while Wilson was president of Princeton University. *Constitutional Government* was written in part to update the earlier book, and in the later work Wilson was much more optimistic about the possibility of presidential leadership of the government. However, *Constitutional Government* does not differ from *Congressional Government* with respect to the fundamental critique of the political science of the American Constitution.

Wilson's *Congressional Government* criticized the form which the United States government had taken by the late nineteenth century, in which the committees of Congress exercised, or seemed to exercise, the real governmental power. The system of congressional government was inferior in point of both democracy and efficiency to the cabinet government system used in Europe, and especially in Britain. In Wilson's rather idealized view, the cabinet system permitted the people, through responsible parties, to lay down the broad outlines of public policy and delegated to the ministers, and to professional civil servants, the task of organizing the details of enforcing and administering that policy.

The Framers of the American Constitution deliberately separated the executive from the legislative authority, so that no one man or small group of men could command both simultaneously. In this way, the liberty and property of the people were given a modicum of security; but the price of that security was potentially a less efficient government. In modern European states, however, the system of cabinet government operated to put exactly the same men at the head of both the legislative and the executive branch:

> In both England and France a ministry composed of the chief officers
> of the executive departments are [sic] constituted at once the leaders of
> legislation and the responsible heads of administration,—a binding link
> between the legislative and executive branches of the government . . .
> bringing legislature and executive side by side in intimate but open
> cooperation.[32]

That system of cabinet government Wilson recommended as bringing
both democracy and efficiency to government.

An article that Wilson published while he was working on *Congressional Government* made the argument even more explicitly than does
the book:

> Cabinet government has in it everything to recommend it. Especially to
> Americans should it commend itself. It is, first of all, the simplest and
> most straightforward system of party government. . . . It is a simple
> legalization of fact; for, as every one knows, we are not free to choose
> between party government or no-party government. . . . It would not
> suffer legislation to skulk in committee closets and caucus conferences.
> . . . Debate would be the breath of its nostrils: for the ministers' tenure
> of office would be dependent on the vindication of their policy.[33]

To Wilson, the graduate student, the real guarantee against governmental abuse of power was not to be found in institutional arrangements
pitting ambition against ambition and interest against interest, but in
lively public debate: "how essential a thing to the preservation of liberty
in the republic is free and unrestricted debate in the representative
body."[34] In contests over what public policies to adopt, "victory must
generally rest with those who are vigorous in debate and strong in
political principle."[35]

Of course, the illusions of his graduate student days did not survive
Wilson's later, more personal knowledge of how politics works. Nevertheless, he continued to admire the greater control over public affairs
exercised by the party leaders of European countries. In an address to the
Virginia State Bar Association in 1897, when he was a professor at
Princeton, Wilson described the American system as "leaderless government."[36] He meant that we are without official leaders—without
leaders who can be held immediately responsible for the action and
policy of the government, alike upon its legislative and upon its administrative side.[37]

This deplorable situation, and Wilson did deplore it at some length in his address, was brought about because

> we have carried the application of the notion that the powers of government must be separated to a dangerous and unheard-of length by thus holding our only national representative, the Executive, at arm's length from Congress, whose very commission it seems to be to represent, not the people, but the communities into which the people are divided.[38]

And he went on to recommend, as he had thirteen years earlier, adoption of the cabinet system of government in America.

Throughout Wilson's career, at least as a political scientist, he sought the twin goals of democracy and efficiency. In 1901, he published an article under the title "Democracy and Efficiency"[39] in which he argued that if a country's legislative authority were democratic it had no reason to fear efficiency in its administrative authority. In that article, Wilson criticized the Framers of the American Constitution for being overly cautious in making dispersion of authority the rule of the government: "We printed the SELF large and the *government* small in almost every administrative arrangement we made."[40] But this was an error:

> It is not a question of the excellence of self-government: it is a question of the method of self-government, and of choosing which word of the compound we shall emphasize in any given case. . . . [I]f only [a democracy] have the principle of representation at the centre of its arrangements, where council is had and policy determined and law made, it can afford to put into its administrative organization any kind of businesslike power or official authority and any kind of discipline as if of a profession that it may think most likely to serve it.[41]

Efficiency of governmental administration had not been necessary in the past, but as, with the coming of the twentieth century, the United States emerged as a world power "[l]eadership and expert organization have become imperative, and our practical sense . . . must be applied to the task of developing them."[42] In *Constitutional Government* Wilson wrote that "governments have their natural evolution and are one thing in one age, another in another."[43] It is clear that he believed that the United States had passed into an age much different from that in which the Constitution was framed, and one in which the ideas and intentions of the Framers had been superseded:

> The makers of the Constitution constructed the federal government upon a theory of checks and balances which was meant to limit the operation of each part and allow to no single part or organ of it a dominating force; but no government can be successfully conducted upon so mechanical a theory.[44]

The problem that the Framers had, however, was that they were saddled, however unconsciously, with an obsolete worldview:

> The government of the United States was constructed upon the Whig theory of political dynamics, which was an unconscious copy of the Newtonian theory of the universe. In our own day, whenever we discuss the structure or development of a thing, whether in nature or in society, we consciously or unconsciously follow Mr. Darwin; but before Mr. Darwin they followed Newton.[45]

In a more enlightened age, once the true character of government as an organic being, rather than a mechanical structure, has been appreciated, the Constitution as the Framers conceived it could not retain its authority. Organisms evolve, constitutions must be adapted to the times. The Constitution of the United States must be subjected to a process of creative reinterpretation to achieve that adaptation:

> Fortunately, the definitions and prescriptions of our constitutional law, though conceived in the Newtonian spirit and upon the Newtonian principle, are sufficiently broad and elastic to allow for the play of life and circumstance. . . . The government of the United States has had a vital and normal organic growth and has proved itself eminently adapted to express the changing temper and purposes of the American people from age to age.[46]

To say this, however, is no different, in Wilson's view, from simply saying (consciously or unconsciously following Darwin) that America has a form of constitutional government. The end of constitutional government, in the Darwinian understanding, is to have no end:

> The object of constitutional government is to bring the active, planning will of each part of the government into accord with the prevailing popular thought and need, and thus make it an impartial instrument of symmetrical national development; and to give to the operation of the government thus shaped under the influence of opinion and adjusted to

the general interest both stability and an incorruptible efficiency. What-ever institutions, whatever practices serve these ends [sic], are neces-sary to such a system; those which do not, or which serve it [sic] imper-fectly, should be dispensed with or bettered.[47]

There is perhaps no better statement of the difference between the old political science and the new concerning the significance of constitu-tional government than this.

If it is so that constitutionalism is nothing other than stability and efficiency in carrying out the national will and expediting the national development, then the task of political science is to determine the necessary conditions for stability and efficiency. The first step toward success in that new political science is the task of organization. The next step is the determination, individually or, better, collectively, of the method best calculated to produce practical results. Finally, the organiza-tion and the methodology must be put to work in the solution of the problem of constitutional government, that is, the problem of stability and efficiency. To that end, the science of politics must produce its corollary, the science of administration.

NOTES

1. *The Federalist*, number 9 (Hamilton), Clinton Rossiter edition (New York: New American Library, 1961), 72–73.

2. *The Federalist*, number 10 (Madison), Rossiter edition, 78.

3. *The Federalist*, number 51 (Madison), Rossiter edition, 322.

4. J. Allen Smith, *The Spirit of American Government: A Study of the Constitution: Its Origin, Influence and Relation to Democracy* (New York: The Macmillan Company, 1907).

5. Charles A. Beard, *An Economic Interpretation of the Constitution of the United States* (New York: The Macmillan Company, 1935). [Originally published by Macmillan, 1913.]

6. Vernon L. Parrington, *The Beginnings of Critical Realism, in America, 1860–1920*, vol. 3 of *Main Currents in American Thought* (New York: Harcourt, Brace & World, Inc., 1958), 406. [This book, which Parrington left unfinished, was first published in 1930.]

7. Parrington, *Beginnings*, 411.

8. Woodrow Wilson, *Congressional Government: A Study in American Politics* (New York: Meridian Books, Inc., 1956), p. 27. [Originally published in 1885.]

9. Wilson, *Congressional Government*, 215.

10. John W. Burgess, *Political Science and Comparative Constitutional*

Law (Boston: Ginn & Company, 1890), vol. 1, 151–152.

11. Burgess, *Political Science*, vol. 1, 153.

12. Burgess, *Political Science*, vol. 1, 264.

13. Burgess, *Political Science*, vol. 2, 6.

14. John W. Burgess, *Recent Changes in American Constitutional Theory* (New York: Columbia University Press, 1923), 43 *ff.*

15. John W. Burgess, *The Reconciliation of Government with Liberty* (New York: Charles Scribner's Sons, 1915), 303.

16. Frank J. Goodnow, *Social Reform and the Constitution* (New York: The Macmillan Company, 1911).

17. Goodnow, *Social Reform*, 1.

18. Goodnow, *Social Reform*, 11.

19. Goodnow, *Social Reform*, 214.

20. Frank J. Goodnow, *Politics and Administration: A Study in Government* (New York: Russell & Russell, 1967), 13. [Originally published in 1900.]

21. Goodnow, *Politics and Administration*, 14.

22. Goodnow, *Politics and Administration*, 21.

23. Goodnow, *Politics and Administration*, 22.

24. Goodnow, *Social Reform*, 331.

25. Goodnow, *Social Reform*, 331–332.

26. Charles E. Merriam, *American Political Ideals: Studies in the Development of American Political Thought, 1865–1917* (New York: The Macmillan Company, 1920), 212–213.

27. Merriam, *American Political Ideals*, 227.

28. Charles E. Merriam, *A History of American Political Theories* (New York: The Macmillan Company, 1902), 96 *ff.*

29. Merriam, *History of American Political Theories*, 75–77, 99–100.

30. Woodrow Wilson, *Constitutional Government in the United States* (New York: Columbia University Press, 1908).

31. Preface to the fifteenth printing of Wilson, *Congressional Government*, 19.

32. Wilson, *Congressional Government*, 97–98.

33. Woodrow Wilson, "Committee or Cabinet Government?" in *College and State: Educational, Literary, and Political Papers (1875–1913)*, ed. by R. S. Baker and W. E. Dodd (New York: Harper & Brothers Publishers, 1925), vol. 1, 114–115. [Originally published in *Overland Monthly*, series 2, vol. 3 (January, 1884).]

34. Wilson, "Committee or Cabinet Government?," 117.

35. Wilson, "Committee or Cabinet Government?," 118.

36. Woodrow Wilson, "Leaderless Government," in *College and State*, vol. 1, 336–359.

37. Wilson, "Leaderless Government," 340.

38. Wilson, "Leaderless Government," 357.

39. Woodrow Wilson, "Democracy and Efficiency," *College and State*,

vol. 1, 396–415. [Originally published in *Atlantic Monthly*, vol. 87 (March 1901).]

40. Wilson, "Democracy and Efficiency," 408.
41. Wilson, "Democracy and Efficiency," 410.
42. Wilson, "Democracy and Efficiency," 411.
43. Wilson, "Democracy and Efficiency," 54.
44. Wilson, "Democracy and Efficiency," 54.
45. Wilson, "Democracy and Efficiency," 54–55.
46. Wilson, "Democracy and Efficiency," 57.
47. Wilson, "Democracy and Efficiency," 14.

Part III

THE NEW POLITICAL SCIENCE

Chapter Seven

PROFESSIONAL ORGANIZATION

One of the characteristics of an academic discipline is that it is an organized body of scholars. Acceptance of the general tenets of pragmatism implies that serious inquirers after facts will organize, because the consensus of the disciplined community of inquiry becomes the surrogate for the truth about the matter. It was almost inevitable that the American Political Science Association should have come into existence.

Learned societies, however, were not the creation of the pragmatists or of the new academic professionals of the late nineteenth and early twentieth centuries. Rather,

> [a]s a promoter and disseminator of knowledge, the learned society has been one of the major institutions of American intellectual life since colonial times. Scientific and humanistic societies have sponsored and organized research, provided opportunities for the exchange and diffusion of knowledge through publications and meetings, and advanced the professional interests of their members.[1]

The first such society, the American Philosophical Society, was founded at Philadelphia in 1769. The American Academy of Arts and Sciences was founded at Boston in 1780. But, until well after the Civil War, the learned societies were not organizations of specialists and professional practitioners. Rather, among "the principal forces behind the creation" of

107

such societies "was the belief that all aspects of learning lay within the province of the educated man."[2] And the educated man of the antebellum period "could, and often did, become a member of several different types of learned societies."[3]

After the Civil War, the replacement of the liberal arts college by the modern university and the rise of specialized academic disciplines overshadowed the various learned societies composed of amateurs and generalists. After the Civil War, "the influence that the regional learned society exerted in the first half of the Civil War" gave way due to "the development of more effective organizations for the promotion of specialized knowledge and the impact of the 'second scientific revolution.'"[4] The first of the specialized professional societies was the American Philological Association, founded in 1869. The two organizations that provided the pattern for and the sponsorship of the A.P.S.A. were both founded in the 1880s, the American Historical Association in 1884 and the American Economic Association in 1885.

At about the same time, learned professions were organizing themselves outside as well as inside of the academy. The first association of medical specialists, the American Ophthalmological Society, was founded in 1864 and nine others were founded between 1868 and 1888.[5] The 1880s also saw the organization of various professional groups in engineering and the natural sciences.[6] The self-identification of professionals in various fields sharply distinguished them, at least in their own consciousness, from those who did not share the self-identification.

The emerging professional societies took the lead in organizing scholarship and academic life.

> Gradually these organizations, each devoted to a specific field of inquiry, began to issue technical and professional journals of their own. By the early twentieth century, many were serving as clearing houses for information on academic employment. Their annual meetings became a locus for the presentation and discussion of the results of research in a language generally intelligible, or at least of interest, only to other experts in the field.[7]

This development has been characterized as "the rearrangement of information networks" resulting from a "sense that information was not flowing efficiently."[8] The traditional learned societies aimed at unification of scientific pursuits, but the specialization that occurred after the Civil War led to a "new kind of pluralism": "As the specialized scientific traditions gained clarity of standards that could be enforced, the internal sanction of the disciplines formed" the channels for the flow of information.[9]

Among the longest-surviving of the learned societies was the American Social Science Association (A.S.S.A.). But that was a relic of an earlier age, dominated by ideas, goals, and methods that were not those of the new political science. Indeed, one historian of the A.S.S.A. has called the members of that association "the last embarrassing practitioners of an extreme form of anti-positivistic social science."[10] The new academic political scientists were among the members of "the transitional generation of social scientists, busily seeking their own legitimation as professionals," who were "eager to forget and even hide" the relationship of their activity to that of the members of the A.S.S.A.[11] Nevertheless, Frank Sanborne, president of the A.S.S.A., wanted the new political scientists to organize within his group; he tried to get them to do so, but he was spurned.[12]

Alternatively, the Academy of Political Science (A.P.S.) could have become the base organization of the new discipline; but it was the creature of John W. Burgess and the Columbia School of Political Science. The A.P.S. had been founded in 1880, and had published America's first political science journal, the *Political Science Quarterly*, since March 1886.[13] In principle, it had been intended to be what the A.P.S.A. became, but at the critical moment it was little more than an alumni association of the Columbia School. Similar academies or associations existed at Johns Hopkins University and elsewhere, but none was independent enough or comprehensive enough to serve as the basis for organizing the whole discipline.

The original scheme from which the A.P.S.A. emerged was a sort of monument to the comparative-historical school of Burgess and Herbert B. Adams. The scheme was to create a society for the comparative study of legislation, meaning, primarily, of administrative law. The letter sent to political scientists throughout the country calling a meeting to organize such a society was signed, among others, by Burgess and, apparently, the entire membership of the Columbia political science department.[14]

The call was made, and, in 1902, a group of about thirty interested persons met in Washington, D.C., to discuss the project. The letter by which the meeting was called referred to an "American Society of Comparative Legislation." However, the opinion of those who attended was that the proposal was too narrowly focused, and that a "National Political Science Association" should be created instead. Those present at the meeting appointed a committee of fifteen members, under Professor Jeremiah Jencks of Cornell University, to draft a broader proposal in consultation with the American Historical Association and the American Economic Association. The Jencks committee was to study the "necessity for a national association that should have for its sphere of interests the entire field of political science."[15]

Jencks's committee met in New York in April 1903 and adopted a resolution that proposed the formation of a society with the entire field of political science as its sphere of interest, "to do work similar to that now being done by the [A.E.A. and A.H.A.] for Economics and History respectively."[16] The committee called for potential members to assemble during the next concurrent annual meetings of the American Historical Association and the American Economics Association. Accordingly, an organizational meeting was held at New Orleans in December 1903, in conjunction with the meetings of the American Historical Association and the American Economics Association:

> Late in the afternoon of December 30, 1903, twenty-five persons gathered in the Tilton Memorial Library at Tulane University and voted the American Political Science Association into existence. With this action, American political science may be said to have shed the chrysalid garb of its formative years and to have donned the full vestments of a learned discipline. . . . Existence of the Association was tangible proof that political science was now an independent discipline; it also served as an active and often effective instrument in promoting that independence.[17]

The delegates had assembled, the proposal had been put to them, and the decision to go ahead had been made. Frank J. Goodnow was elected president and Westel W. Willoughby secretary-treasurer, and a constitution was written and adopted. The formal organization was complete, but the real work of organizing was left to the officers and committees. Having done a good day's work, the organizational meeting of the A.P.S.A. adjourned.

Over the course of the next month, Willoughby, as secretary-treasurer, prepared a letter reporting what had been done and soliciting membership in the A.P.S.A., not only on the part of academic political scientists, but of lawyers, politicians, public administrators, "and, in general, of all those interested in the scientific study of the great and increasingly important questions of practical and theoretical politics."[18] These efforts enlisted 205 regular members and nine life members for the new Association. The executive council subsequently met and established within the Association nine sections:

> Comparative Legislation; International Law and Diplomacy; Public Administration; Municipal Government; Constitutional Law; Colonies and Dependencies; Political Parties; Political Theory; and Instruction in Political Science.[19]

In Chicago, Illinois, on the morning of 28 December 1904, Professor Frank J. Goodnow, president of the American Political Science Association, called to order the first full-scale public meeting of the organization. The business meeting was short, its main activity being to hear Willoughby's report. The meeting did, however, adopt two resolutions on the subject of comparative legislation: one commending the Library of Congress, the other commending the Agriculture and Commerce Departments for their respective efforts in compiling and indexing foreign legislation. The meeting elected officers for the following year, including, once again, Goodnow as president and Willoughby as secretary-treasurer. The 1904 meeting was the first at which scholarly papers were presented; there were twelve in all, ranging in topic from colonial policies to tendencies in railroad taxation law.

The founding of the Association represented achievement by the new political science of the status of a profession. The graduate schools and the *Quarterly* already existed. Now,

> [w]ith the Association, there came the remaining—and hitherto absent—formal characteristics of a learned discipline: an official organization, an officialdom, an official journal, and regular, officially prescribed meeting of the membership.[20]

Most of the members of the association that was founded in 1903–1904 were academics who were also members of the American Historical Association or the American Economic Association, or both. A good number of the founding members were faculty members or graduates of either Columbia or Johns Hopkins. Although Burgess did not participate in the activities of the new association, the first president, Frank J. Goodnow, was Burgess's own choice to teach public administration at Columbia. On the other hand, Goodnow, and most of the active members of the new group, stood well to the left of Burgess. Even as the American Economic Association had a program—advance toward some form of socialism—the American Political Science Association had a program—

implementation of progressive social reform measures. The "science" of which they were the official spokesmen was not neutral in that regard.

The first four presidents of the A.P.S.A. (Goodnow, Bryce, Lowell and Wilson) "had a strong belief in common that political studies must have direct relevance to practical politics."[21] In this the leadership and membership were united in a distrust of political theory, which, apparently at least, had no immediate application to the reform politics of the day. "[T]he belief of most of those who founded the association was that a systematic understanding of Politics (as a necessary prelude to reform) had been bedeviled by excessive discussion of how they should work."[22] In the new association

> [a] firm separation was demanded between normative and factual propositions. "Ends" were broadly a political question for popular electoral decision; "means" towards those ends, and the knowledge that would contribute towards making these means efficient—these could be a much-more-than-less scientific question.[23]

The Association's official journal, the *American Political Science Review* began publication in November 1906. One effect of publication of the *Review* was that a certain homogeneity of opinion about the methods, purposes, and conclusions of political science was thereby assured.

As professionalization of the discipline proceeded apace, members needed publication to enhance their credibility and advance their careers. Established political scientists could afford to flout the official understanding, but younger men had to accommodate that view or find themselves practically excluded from the journal and hence from the profession. In this way, as Somit and Tanenhaus have observed, "the *Review* molded no less than it mirrored."[24]

The organization, journal, and other trappings of academic respectability, also fostered another requisite of a learned discipline—a common state of mind. If a discipline is to flourish, its practitioners must be in general agreement about their subject matter, their techniques, and the interests and behavior appropriate to the practice of their profession. Although the common state of mind was formed first, the vastly expanded opportunities for contact and communication afforded by the newborn Association would do much both to strengthen and to shape the views shared by its members.[25]

Much of the character of the new discipline of political science can be learned from a study of the early years of the A.P.S.A. The organization of the association declares the interests and priorities of the early membership. The presidential addresses were largely devoted to expounding the meaning, purpose, and methods of the new discipline. The offices were held by the men for whose achievements the membership had the highest regard.

The presidential address of Frank J. Goodnow, delivered at that 1904 meeting, was entitled: "The Work of the American Political Science Association." Although resisting the temptation to define "political science," Goodnow did say that it was the science of the State, both at rest and in action. "Inasmuch, however, as it is the State in action which causes the phenomena of the greatest practical concern to the individual," the work of the A.P.S.A. would be concerned with the active State, and, in particular, with "the various operations necessary to the realization of the State will."[26] That subject, Goodnow asserted, divided itself into three parts: the expression of the State will; the content of the State will; and the execution of the State will. By far the largest part of Goodnow's address, and presumably, the largest part of the work of the A.P.S.A., was concerned with the third part of the subject, the execution of the State will, or its equivalent, public administration.

The first great work of the Association, in Goodnow's scheme, was to be the accumulation, indexing, and cross-referencing, of statistical material, especially dealing with municipal administration. Such a task would, "even if tolerably done, have amply justified the addition of the American Poltical Science Association to the already long list of societies now in existence."[27] In Goodnow's understanding, "the study of administration is of the greatest importance," and the compilation of raw data for such a study was "a most important work for this organization to take up."[28]

Secondarily, in addition to this "tangible and measurable work" was the opportunity the Association would provide for professional interaction. Given the composition of the original body, it is not surprising that Goodnow first refers to the interaction of men of practice—politicians, administrators, lawyers—with men of theory—academic political scientists. The meeting and interaction of teachers of politics was the aspect of the work of the A.P.S.A. that Goodnow saved for his penultimate paragraph. "The meetings of this Association ought also to have the greatest value to those of us who are engaged in the work of teaching," he declared, "For only by personal contact with colaborers in the broad field we are essaying to cultivate, can we learn what is being done at other institutions."[29] But that was an important part of the Association's

work, and one that provided professional satisfaction as well as intellectual companionship: "There is none of us, I am sure, who did not feel
that the establishment of the [A.P.S.A.] offered us an advantage which
we had long envied the historian and the economist."[30]

Albert Shaw, in his presidential address delivered in December 1906,
took up Goodnow's theme of the work of the Association. His address
began where Goodnow's left off, that is, with the function of professional self-definition that the organization performed by its mere existence. The establishment of the A.P.S.A., Shaw suggested, was justified
by "the emergence upon this field of study and action of a body of
trained and competent men like Professor Goodnow himself, who are
primarily political scientists rather than historians or economists."[31] The
significance of such self-definition in the process of professionalization
appears much more clearly in Shaw's address than it had in Goodnow's:

> The logical differentiation of the subject matter is one thing, and the
> appearance of a group of men dealing by preference with that material
> is something quite different. With us in the United States this develop-
> ment of a trained body of political scientists is a comparatively recent
> fact.[32]

It soon becomes clear that the "trained body" of political scientists
comprised most importantly specialists in public administration.

The Association, in Shaw's view, was committed to the practical
application of the findings of political science. The members "are both
willing and eager to see the results of their scientific study . . . converted
to the ends of statesmanship."[33] He proposed, therefore, that the Association itself sponsor research that would be useful to active politicians,
promising results that "will be of practical benefit to the perplexed
legislator in his hour of need."[34] Shaw apparently had an extensive
program of such research in mind:

> A series of inquiries ably conducted under the auspices of this Associa-
> tion, carried on with diligence and energy, both without bias and in the
> purely scientific spirit, might come to have an almost monumental
> character and importance. . . . [T]here will be a very general agreement
> that this Association can render an extremely useful service to the
> country, without departing in the smallest degree from its scientific
> methods of work.[35]

One thing that is not immediately clear is who were the perplexed legislators who would be so grateful for assistance in their hour of need. They must have been enlightened fellows, indeed, for they presumably shared in the general conviction that scientific students, like those who unite in the carrying on of organizations like the A.P.S.A., have a large common stock of sincerity and of intelligence, and possess a habit of mind which checks controversial attitudes and faddish enthusiasms, where questions of clear fact and of scientific bearing are essentially involved.[36] They were also presumed not to care whether the particular dispassionate scientists were Republicans or Democrats, socialists or individualists.

The apparent naiveté of President Shaw may perhaps be attributed to excessive zeal of the professional spirit. Only three years later, in his own presidential address, A. Lawrence Lowell, who was more closely associated than Shaw with both academic political science and practical politics, admitted that "active men in political life tend to disregard suggestions from academic sources even when based upon a study of results."[37]

The notion of political science, and especially the A.P.S.A., in the public service permeates the official pronouncements of the Association's presidents up until the First World War despite the evidence that the public and its representatives were not particularly interested. But the notion was not always treated as sanguinely as it was by Shaw. James Bryce, in his presidential address, delivered in 1908, addressed himself in part to the question: "What help can [political science] render to the world by placing its facts and conclusions at the service of statesmen and citizens?"[38] "What is the use of Political Science?" he asked, and, "Can it be made to serve the practical needs of the time?"[39]

Somewhat more realistic than Shaw's estimation of the deference politicians would show to the results of scientific study was Bryce's assessment that political scientists "must not be expected to provide authoritative solutions for current problems and controversies."[40] "Doubtless," he admits, "the professors of the science are ready to prescribe." But neither Bryce nor practical politicians, expected the professors to put science above party, for "whenever Party comes in at the door Science flies out at the window."[41] And he admonished the assembled professionals to "[c]herish no vain hopes of introducing the certitude or the authority of science into politics."[42]

While at annual meetings the Association's presidents engaged in flights of fancy like Shaw's, the members settled into the business of academic professionalism. The number of members showed steady growth, increasing from 214 in 1904 to 1350 in 1910 and 1462 in 1915.[43] The A.P.S.A. had become precisely that "association of people who supposedly have the knowledge for which the [academic] degree was acquired and who, as a group are presumably interested in advancing it" that is one of the characteristics of professionalized science.[44]

Professionalized science shared in what has been called the "culture of professionalism," built around the self-perception (and self-promotion) of the professional practitioners. The stereotypical professional saw himself as part of an emergent leader class in American society:

> He was self-reliant, independent, ambitious, and mentally organized. He structured a life and a career around noble aims and purposes, including the ideal of moral obligation. But most importantly, the professional person absolutely protected his precious autonomy against all assailants, not in the name of an irrational egotism but in the name of a special grasp of the universe and a special place in it.[45]

The organized professions benefited not only from the scholarly pursuits of the members, but also from an emotional commitment that bound the members to the community of scholars. The collectivization and systematization of inquiry within the profession benefited the member by giving him access to a more trustworthy explanation of the world:

> The independent inquirer had to be replaced by collective inquiry for fundamentally epistemological reasons: in a highly interdependent society the mind of the isolated investigator seemed powerless to encompass the whole, and therefore unable to comprehend even the part . . . The success or professionalization was . . . the consequence of a profound change in the conditions of satisfactory explanation.[46]

The American Political Science Association, as the corporate entity within which inquiry into the political things was to take place, was the response of the new political science to that epistemological revolution.

NOTES

1. John Voss, "The Learned Society in American Intellectual Life," foreword to Alexandra Oleson and Sanborn C. Brown, eds., *The Pursuit of Knowledge in the Early American Republic: American Scientific and Learned*

Societies from Colonial Times to the Civil War (Baltimore, Md.: The Johns
Hopkins University Press, 1976.), vii.

2. Voss, "Learned Society," vii.

3. Voss, "Learned Society," viii.

4. Voss, "Learned Society," viii.

5. Burton J. Bledstein, *The Culture of Professionalism: The Middle Class
and the Development of Higher Education in America* (New York: W.W.
Norton & Company, Inc., 1976), 85.

6. Bledstein, *Culture of Professionalism*, 86.

7. Voss, "Learned Society," ix.

8. A. Hunter Dupree, "The National Pattern of Learned Societies, 1769–
1863" in *Pursuit of Knowledge*, 31.

9. Dupree, "National Pattern," 31.

10. Thomas L. Haskell, *The Emergence of Professional Social Science*
(Urbana: University of Illinois Press, 1977), 8.

11. Haskell, *Emergence*, 8.

12. Haskell, *Emergence*, 230–231.

13. John W. Burgess, *Reminiscences of an American Scholar* (Morningside
Heights, N.Y.: Columbia University Press, 1934), 200–201.

14. "The Organization of the American Political Science Association,"
Proceedings of the American Political Science Association, vol. 1 (1904): 5.

15. "Organization," 5–6; see also: Albert Somit and Joseph Tannenhaus,
*The Development of American Political Science: From Burgess to Behavioral-
ism* (Boston: Allyn and Bacon, Inc., 1967) 51.

16. "Organization," 8–9.

17. Somit and Tannenhaus, *Development*, 50.

18. Westel W. Willoughby, "Report of the Secretary for the Year 1904,"
Proceedings of the American Political Science Association, vol. 1 (1904): 27–
28.

19. Willoughby, "Report," 30.

20. Somit and Tannenhaus, *Development*, 50.

21. Bernard Crick, *The American Science of Politics: Its Origin and
Conditions* (Berkeley: University of California Press, 1964) 101.

22. Crick, *American Science*, 101. The antecedent of "they" is "politics," a
plural noun according to British usage.

23. Crick, *American Science*, 101.

24. Somit and Tannenhaus, *Development*, 54.

25. Somit and Tannenhaus, *Development*, 50.

26. Frank J. Goodnow, "The Work of the American Political Science
Association," *Proceedings of the American Political Science Association*, vol. 1
(1904): 37.

27. Goodnow, "Work," 45.

28. Goodnow, "Work," 44–45.

29. Goodnow, "Work," 46.

30. Goodnow, "Work," 46.

31. Albert Shaw, "Presidential Address," *American Political Science Review*, vol. 1 (1907): 178.

32. Shaw, "Presidential Address," 178.

33. Shaw, "Presidential Address," 180.

34. Shaw, "Presidential Address," 181.

35. Shaw, "Presidential Address," 181.

36. Shaw, "Presidential Address," 186.

37 A. Lawrence Lowell, "The Physiology of Politics," *The American Political Science Review*, vol. 4 (1910): 4.

38. James Bryce, "The Relations of Political Science to History and to Practice," *The American Political Science Review*, vol. 3 (1909): 4.

39. Bryce, "Relations," 11.

40. Bryce, "Relations," 16.

41. Bryce, "Relations," 16–17.

42. Bryce, "Relations," 18.

43. Somit and Tannenhaus, *Development*, 55.

44. Nathan Reingold, "Definitions and Speculations: The Professionalization of Science in America in the Nineteenth Century," in *Pursuit of Knowledge*, 37.

45. Bledstein, *Culture of Professionalism*, 92.

46. Haskell, *Emergence*, 237.

Chapter Eight

METHODOLOGY

The history of American political science since the appointment of Burgess and the founding of the Columbia School of Political Science has been, to a large extent, the history of a discipline looking for a methodology. John W. Burgess and Herbert Baxter Adams, the mentors of the founding generation of the new discipline, brought from Germany the method of the seminar—the historical-comparative method. The assumptions that underlay that method have been exposed in previous chapters. Historical and comparative study of political institutions made especial sense if all political history was the history of progress, if the various nation-states experienced the same stages of historical development, and if some nation-states progressed more rapidly than others, and therefore showed the direction in which history was moving.

Among the earliest graduate students to work under Burgess and Adams were those who transformed the historical-comparative method by applying it to questions of administration, rather than of politics, and by applying it to governments as they actually functioned rather than to constitutions, statutes, and documents. The men behind this transformation were influenced mainly by the Progressive movement—they wanted a political science with practical application to the problem of political reform.

Frank J. Goodnow was a graduate student under Burgess, and he later led the revolution at Columbia that made administration the main concern of political science. Goodnow stressed the practical value of the historical-comparative method. In one book, for example, he sets out

> to state in the first place what is the program of political and social re-
> form proposed by most modern progressive countries which have been
> called upon to solve the problems the American people will soon be
> called upon to solve.[1]

A necessary course of political evolution is followed by every nation-state, and the great desideratum of political science is to be able to learn from the most progressive States, i.e., those that have progressed the farthest along that evolutionary course. Allied with Goodnow was Woodrow Wilson who, like Goodnow, was primarily interested in administration and who was even more critical than Goodnow of the Burgess-Adams form of historical-comparative study.

Both of those methodological schools—the Burgess-Adams school and the Goodnow-Wilson school—professed a primary concern with systematization of knowledge. An envious eye was cast, this time under the influence of the pragmatists, upon the physical sciences, and the rigor there achieved. More and more the state seemed a laboratory in which it was possible to conduct controlled experiments.

The attempt to create a truly scientific method for the study of politics was a third phase of methodological concern. Where Wilson, Goodnow, and others of their persuasion sought to put political science in closer touch with reality by studying the functions of government rather than the structure, the third group sought to replace a merely descriptive political science with one more quantitatively based.

What each of the methodological schools had in common with the others was the faith in progress that was instilled in turn by the German science of politics, by pragmatism and the apparent success of the natural sciences, and by the reform politics of the Progressive Era. Dwight Waldo explained the tendency of political science, and, indeed, the social sciences in general, to attempt to emulate the physical sciences in the following way: everyone desires progress; but progress, to be recognized as such, must be toward some goal; there is no generally agreed upon goal for politics, hence no way of measuring progress; but the natural sciences have made what everyone agrees is progress; so, to ensure progress in politics and society, we must imitate the methods of natural science.[2] Waldo described how the students and reformers of politics went about making politics scientific:

> The students by engaging in a new and recondite branch of inquiry called Scientific Methodology, and the reformers either by applying current conceptions of scientific method or by the simpler method of putting a scientific wrapper on old nostrums.[3]

The second chapter of Johann K. Bluntschli's treatise on general state theory,[4] a treatise which was extremely influential in the early years of American academic political science, treats the subject of methodology. The "authorised" English translation renders the chapter title as "Scientific Methods," although the Americans who knew the work in German probably understood the title as "Methods of the Discipline." Bluntschli admitted two correct and two incorrect methods for the study of politics. The correct methods were the philosophical and the historical; the incorrect methods were their corresponding corrupt forms, the ideological and the empirical.

According to Bluntschli's exposition, the philosophical method is not mere abstract speculation, but the uniting of ideas and reality. It "starts from the knowledge of the human mind, and from that point of view considers the revelation of the spirit of man in history."[5] The historical method—Bluntschli's method—he describes as comprising the recognition, explanation, and interpretation of the "organic development of national life and the moral idea as revealed in its history."[6]

The advantages of the historical method, according to Bluntschli, lay in the "abundance and positive character of its results."[7] The positive results to which Bluntschli refers are evidently knowledge of "the different stages of development which mankind has lived through" and knowledge of "the ways in which various nations have taken part in the various tasks of the human race."[8] Because political science is concerned only or especially with the modern State, the historical and comparative method has the positive result of revealing "the value of different peoples . . . determined in general by their share in the progress of political civilisation."[9]

Heinrich von Treitschke, following and correcting the supposed errors in Bluntschli's teaching, understood political science as applied history:

The task of Politics is threefold. It must first seek to discover . . . the fundamental idea of the State. It must then discover historically what the nations have desired in their political life, what they have created, what they have accomplished, and how they have accomplished it. This will lead on to the third object, the discovery of certain historic laws and the setting forth of some moral imperatives.[10]

Treitschke had only one major complaint against Bluntschli's theories: "Scientific politics itself, as Bluntschli represented it, is still hampered by the old theory of Natural Law."[11] Treitschke thought it possible to put political science, that is, applied history, on a more scientific basis than had hitherto been known. Political science, he wrote,

must follow the methods of scientific history and draw deductions from empirical observations. But these methods are far more complicated than the simple, straightforward manner of reaching conclusions which is proper to the Natural Sciences. . . . The scientific historian must work backwards from results, which are indeed the very elements of his craft. . . . If history were an exact science, the future of governments might stand revealed.[12]

What prevents political science, as applied history, from becoming an exact science is the "riddle of personality," that is, the role of individual men in political history. But, in this paragraph, the object of political science is revealed: political science is the discipline that distinguishes the stages of evolution through which the State has passed; an exact political science would accurately predict the stages of that evolution which are yet to come.

John W. Burgess, who was responsible for the importation of the German science of politics into the American university, consciously adopted the German historical and comparative methods. This is evident in Burgess's most important book, *Political Science and Comparative Constitutional Law*.[13] Burgess's book, however, does not include any discussion of the methodology of political science as such.

Expositions of the historical-comparative method are to be found in some of the introductory textbooks of the early twentieth century. James W. Garner, who earned his Ph.D. at Columbia in 1902, published his *Introduction to Political Science* in 1910. In the section of that work dealing with the methods of political science, Garner described the historical method as a variant of the comparative method. Garner approvingly cited a French student of public law when he describes the comparative method as one that "discovers the 'general current' which runs through the whole body of constitutions and upon which experience has set the stamp of approval."[14] Garner further specified the canons of comparison

> then most perfect of which is the process of difference by which two polities identical in every particular except one are compared with a view to discovering the effect of the differing factor. Thus two states are compared which are similar as regards their natural wealth, legal systems, racial conditions, etc., but one of which maintains a protective trade system. If, therefore, one is found to be prosperous and the other not, a general conclusion is postulated with regard to the effect of commercial polities upon the national prosperity. The method of indirect difference compares two classes of "instances" which agree in nothing but the presence of a factor on one side and its absence on the other. . . . By the method of agreement two polities wholly different with the exception of two common factors may be compared.[15]

Each of the three methods presents some obvious problems. To Garner's credit, he recognized that the last two involve logical difficulties with respect to causes and effects. He seemed untroubled by the prospective difficulty of finding two or more polities so substantially identical as to permit comparison.

That difficulty, of course, would be at least partly overcome by application of the historical method as a variant of the comparative, for one would thereby examine a single political unit over time. Moreover, that method brings in review the great political movements of the past, traces the organic development of the national life, inquires into the growth of political ideas from their inception to their realization in objective institutions, discovers the moral idea as revealed in history and thereby points out the way of progress.[16] The historical method therefore copes with the principal problem of the comparative method generally, that is, the dearth of identical States to compare, and, at the same time, reveals the course of progress.

The initial critique of the historical-comparative school within American political science was directed not at the methodology but at the choice of data. The chief critic was Woodrow Wilson, who contended that Burgess and his students and followers were too much concerned with the formal legal structures of states and too little with their actual workings. Wilson began his critique in a review of Burgess's *Political*

Science and Comparative Constitutional Law.[17] The faults of Burgess's work, according to Wilson,

> [s]tated in the plainest words that come to hand, they consist in a mechanical and incorrect style, a dogmatic spirit, and a lack of insight into institutions as detailed expressions of life, not readily consenting to be broadly and positively analyzed and classified.[18]

Nevertheless, Wilson generally approved the broadly historical part of Burgess's book, reserving his harshest comments for the comparative section. "Almost all that is most individual and important in Mr. Burgess's thought," he wrote, "lies within the first portion of his work, which deals with the greater topics of political science."[19] Approving Burgess's theoretical construction, Wilson objected that it was "in the application of it to the actual facts of political life, the actual phenomena of state growth, that difficulty enters."[20]

Wilson accepted Burgess's distinction between the law and the facts of political life, but thought the ascertainment of the facts was more problematic than Burgess was willing to admit. "For the facts have to be determined; and while it is generally easy enough to determine what the law is, political fact is subtle and elusive, not to be caught up whole in any formula."[21] Burgess, according to Wilson, failed to make a proper distinction between the law and the facts, and confused the method of the jurist with that of the political scientist. In contrast to the logical method of the jurist, according to Wilson, the method of political science "is the interpretation of life; its instrument is insight, a nice understanding of subtle, unformulated conditions."[22] Interestingly enough, Wilson equated the juristic method with the scientific; Burgess, he complained, "does not write in the language of literature, but in the language of science. The sentences . . . are simply ordered pieces of statements."[23]

Wilson himself believed the proper method of political science to be comparative, descriptive, and analytical. His statements on methodology did not vary much between his first book, *Congressional Government*, which was also his doctoral dissertation, and the time he left academic life for a more direct involvement in politics. In *Congressional Government*, Wilson began by asserting that previous accounts of Congress and of the American system of government all began with the text of the Constitution, and proceeded as if that document had finally settled the questions of how the government was to operate. Wilson, by contrast, set out to describe how Congress actually operated. No one before him, Wilson said, had

> examined minutely and at length that internal organization of Congress which determines its methods of legislation, which shapes its means of governing the executive departments, which contains in it the whole mechanism whereby the policy of the country is in all points directed, and which is therefore an essential branch of constitutional study.[24]

This, Wilson argued, was essential because:

> Anyone who is unfamiliar with what Congress actually does and how it does it, with all its duties and all its occupations, with all its devices of management and resources of power, is very far from a knowledge of the constitutional system under which we live; and to every one who knows these things that knowledge is very near.[25]

Political science, properly constituted to arrive at real political knowledge, therefore ought to concern itself with observation and description of the actual working of institutions rather than with speculative theory or with the legal structure of government.

Nearly twenty-seven years after writing *Congressional Government*, Wilson served as president of the American Political Science Association. His presidential address was entitled "The Law and the Facts."[26] In that address, Wilson declared:

> I take the science of politics to be the accurate and detailed observation of these processes by which the lessons of experience are brought into the field of consciousness, transmuted into active purposes, put under the scrutiny of discussion sifted, and at last given determinate form in law.[27]

According to Wilson, the proper method of political science was subjective, even intuitive. The political scientist must become familiar with the political community he is studying, and with its culture, so that he can identify the "facts" of political life within that community:

> The student of political science must furnish the [statesmanship of thought], out of his full store of truth, discovered by patient inquiry, dispassionate exposition, fearless analysis, and frank inference. He must spread a dragnet for all the facts, and must then look upon them steadily and look upon them whole.[28]

For his descriptive study of politics, Wilson rejected the name "political science." "I do not like the term political science," he wrote, "Human relationships, whether in the family or in the state. . . . are not in any proper sense the subject-matter of science."[29]

Another of the realist-descriptive school was Wilson's immediate predecessor as president of the A.P.S.A., A. Lawrence Lowell. Lowell compared the study of the body politic to the study of the human body. The historical-comparative method as practiced by Burgess he likened to the study of anatomy: that is, it was concerned with the structure of the organism. But the proper methodology of political science he likened to physiology: that is, it is concerned with how the organism works and how its internal organs are related. He used his presidential address "to urge a more thorough investigation of the physiology of politics."[30]

Lowell's physiology had to be practiced under certain handicaps, however. First, in studying the physiology of politics "we are limited by the impossibility of experiment."[31] As a substitute, Lowell urged careful, penetrating, accurate observation. The laboratory of political physiology Lowell, predictably enough, found in "the real world of public life."[32]

At the same time, however, there was a growing tendency within the discipline toward adoption of a methodology more nearly resembling the methodology of the natural sciences. The first steps in this direction were taken by survey researchers, essentially following Lowell's admonition closely to observe the real world of politics, studying parties and elections. But the attempt to formulate a more scientific methodology led some political scientists to redefine their subject matter to facilitate quantification. Foremost among this group was Arthur F. Bentley, whose book, *The Process of Government*,[33] published in 1908, carried, on a separate page following the title page, the legend: "This Book is An Attempt to Fashion a Tool."[34]

Bentley's "scientific" political science defined its subject matter differently from the political science it meant to replace. Burgess, following his German teachers, had defined his subject matter as "the State." Wilson, too, although objecting to the dogmatic aspects of the German science of politics, allowed "the state" to stand for the subject matter of politics. But Bentley wrote that the subject matter was

> first, last, and always activity, action, "something doing," the shunting by some men of other men is conduct along changed lines, the gathering of forces to overcome resistance to such alterations, or the dispersal of one grouping of forces by another grouping. The writing and talking

and speech-making are activity just as much as any of the other facts I have mentioned.[35]

Before there can be a science of politics, Bentley asserted, "[w]e must get our raw material before us in the form of purposive action, valued in terms of other purposive action."[36] Bentley agreed with Wilson that the raw material for the study of government was not to be found in constitutions and law books, but he was equally adamant that it was not to "be found in the 'character of the people,' in their specific 'feelings' or 'thoughts,' in their 'hearts' or 'minds.'"[37] That is, it was not to be found where Wilson was looking for it.

Bentley adopted language calculated to give the impression of a science as rigorous and precise as physics or chemistry. Political science is to have an instrument, as the instrument of physics is the microscope: "We have no microscope of glass and brass; we must make one by concentrating attention at the right spots."[38] Some of the activities which are to be the subject matter of our science are difficult to discern: "we may draw an analogy between them and molecular motion."[39] Others are on a larger scale, are "palpable": "the palpable or external activity corresponds with molar motion."[40]

The activity that is to be investigated by Bentley's political science methodology is the activity of men in the mass. "The activity is always the activity of men," but "[h]uman society is always a mass of men, and nothing else."[41] But the mass of men is made up of overlapping groups, that is, subsidiary masses. "The whole of social life in all its phases can be stated in such groups of active men."[42] Because the groups overlap, one man may belong to groups that have conflicting interests. In that case, to discuss the conflict between the groups and to discuss the process by which the one man forms his opinion are but two approaches to discussing the same phenomenon.[43] The activity of the individual, in forming an opinion, corresponds to molecular motion in physics; the activity of the groups, in conflicting, corresponds to molar motion in physics.

Bentley's methodology did not permit the subject matter of political science to be distinguished at the outset from other activities that were not part of that subject matter, which from the point of view of the nonscientist might seem to be social, religious, or economic, rather than political.

Instead, we shall plunge into any phenomena or set of phenomena belonging to the roughly recognized field of government, be it Congress

in session, a town meeting, a murderer's trial, a ballot-box manipulation at election time, or a mass meeting communicating the oracles of
the age. If any of these things lead us to interesting paths we shall be
prepared to follow them, heedless of definitions.[44]

The method of Bentley is less confident of its subject matter than the
method of either Burgess or Wilson. But its author has greater confidence in his, and his method's, manipulative ability than either of his
predecessors. Before the data can be manipulated, however, they must be
measured. "It is impossible to attain scientific treatment of material that
will not submit itself to measurement in some form. Measure conquers
chaos."[45] Measurement, in turn, implies quantification. Modern natural
science as we know it, and as Bentley knew it, involves the expression of
the relationship between data in quantitative form. Bentley was aware
that, by and large, a commonsense view of political phenomena regards
them as impervious to quantification. However,

> quantities are present in every bit of political life. There is no political
> process that is not a balancing of quantity against quantity. There is not
> a law that is passed that is not the expression of force and force in ten-
> sion. . . . Understanding these phenomena means measuring the ele-
> ments that have gone into them.[46]

Be this as it may, however, Bentley never quite deals with the problem of
measurement of political phenomena.

The groups whose activities constitute the political phenomena
comprise different numbers of members. The number of adherents or
group members is surely quantifiable. But "[n]umber alone may not
secure dominance."[47] There are at least two other factors to be taken into
account: intensity and technique. To these may be added: public opinion,
leadership, and individual and group abilities. Although Bentley enumer-
ates all of these, he does not indicate how he would go about quantifying
them, or balancing the measured quantity of one factor against the
measured quantity of another.

The way in which this sort of problem is customarily dealt with in
academic treatises is to assert that the author has provided the framework
within which a problem can be solved and that it is for others to work out
the details. Bentley does not disappoint the reader who is familiar with
such works:

> But, of course, this work . . . is not to be the work of a day or a year,

but of many men through many years, perhaps through many generations. Toilsome observation and analysis, real laboratory work with society, will be necessary for it. . . . To enable this work of establishing reliable statements of the group facts to make more rapid progress, the method by which the dross can be eliminated and the compounds broken down must be clearly worked out. [48]

Significantly, the book that began by announcing itself as an attempt to formulate a tool refers in its final sentence to "whatever tools of method we devise for the tasks that are to be done."[49]

The common element among the Burgess group, the Wilson group, and the Bentley group of political scientists is the search for a method, a technique, the application of which will guarantee the results of the inquiry. The standard history of the discipline of political science in America treats the groups as disjunctive[50] because it was written within the context established by that controversy. From another perspective however, the controversy took place within a consensus, and that consensus held that, in addition to a coherent body of scholars, an organized community of inquiry, the new science of politics needed a method or technique of its own.

NOTES

1. Frank J. Goodnow, *Social Reform and the Constitution* (New York: The Macmillan Company, 1911), 5.

2. Dwight Waldo, *The Administrative State: A Study of the Political Theory of American Public Administration* (New York: The Ronald Press Company, 1948), 16–21.

3. Waldo, *Administrative State*, 20–21.

4. Johann K. Bluntschli, *Allgemeine Statslehre* (part I of *Lehre vom, modernen Stat*) (1852). *The Theory of the State*, authorized English translation from the sixth German edition, translated by D. G. Ritchie, P. E. Matheson, and R. Lodge (Oxford: The Clarendon Press, 1885), 5.

5. Bluntschli, *Theory of the State*, 7. NB, "human mind" and "spirit of man" are translations of essentially the same German phrase.

6. Bluntschli, *Theory of the State*, 7.

7. Bluntschli, *Theory of the State*, 7.

8. Bluntschli, *Theory of the State*, 11.

9. Bluntschli, *Theory of the State*, 11.

10. Heinrich von Treitschke, *Politics*, edited and translated by Hans Kohn (New York: Harcourt, Brace & World, Inc., 1963), xix.

11. Treitschke, *Politics*, xix.

12. Treitschke, *Politics*, xix.

13. John W. Burgess, *Political Science and Comparative Constitutional Law* (2 volumes) (Boston: Ginn & Company, 1890).

14. James W. Garner, *Introduction to Political Science* (New York: American Book Company, 1910), 26, citing an author named Saleilles.

15. Garner, *Introduction*, 27–28.

16. Garner, *Introduction*, 28–29, citing Bluntschli.

17. Woodrow Wilson, "A System of Political Science and Constitutional Law," in R. S. Baker and W. E. Dodd, eds., *College and State: Educational, Literary and Political Papers (1875–1913)* (New York: Harper & Brothers Publishers, 1925), vol. I, 187–197. [Originally published in *Atlantic Monthly* 67 (1891), 694–699.]

18. Wilson, "System," 188.

19. Wilson, "System," 189.

20. Wilson, "System," 192.

21. Wilson, "System," 193.

22. Wilson, "System," 195.

23. Wilson, "System," 196.

24. Woodrow Wilson, *Congressional Government: A Study in American Politics* (New York: Meridian Books, Inc., 1956), 56. [Originally published in 1885.]

25. Wilson, *Congressional Government*, 56.

26. Woodrow Wilson, "The Law and the Facts," *American Political Science Review* 5 (1911): 1–11.

27. Wilson, "Law and Facts," 2.

28. Wilson, "Law and Facts," 8.

29. Wilson, "Law and Facts," 11–12.

30. A. Lawrence Lowell, "The Physiology of Politics," *American Political Science Review*, vol. 4 (1910): 1–2.

31. Lowell, "Physiology of Politics," 7.

32. Lowell, "Physiology of Politics," 8.

33. Arthur F. Bentley, *The Process of Government* (Chicago: University of Chicago Press, 1908). [Photographically reproduced and reissued, Cambridge, Mass.: Belknap Press of Harvard University Press, 1967.]

34. Bentley, *Process of Government*, vii.

35. Bentley, *Process of Government*, 176.

36. Bentley, *Process of Government*, 179.

37. Bentley, *Process of Government*, 179–180.

38. Bentley, *Process of Government*, 184.

39. Bentley, *Process of Government*, 185.

40. Bentley, *Process of Government*, 185.

41. Bentley, *Process of Government*, 185.

42. Bentley, *Process of Government*, 204.

43. Bentley, *Process of Government*, 204.

45. Bentley, *Process of Government*, 200.
46. Bentley, *Process of Government*, 202.
47. Bentley, *Process of Government*, 215.
48. Bentley, *Process of Government*, 482.
49. Bentley, *Process of Government*, 484.
50. Albert Somit and Joseph Tannenhaus, *The Development of American Political Science: From Burgess to Behavioralism* (Boston: Allyn and Bacon, Inc., 1967), 63–79.

Chapter Nine

PUBLIC ADMINISTRATION

Political science, wrote Woodrow Wilson, is over 2200 years old, but the science of administration "is a birth of our own century, almost of our own generation."[1] Moreover, "it is a foreign science, speaking very little of the language of English or American principle . . . developed by French and German professors."[2] The importation and adaptation of the "science" of public administration to America was largely the work of Wilson and of Frank J. Goodnow of Columbia. The introduction of public administration into the university was one of the premier accomplishments of the new American political science.

Public administration became a subject of study in the new departments of political science at just the right moment for the Progressive movement. Progressivist ideology gave efficiency in government second place only to democracy itself. If political scientists studied various administrative techniques, and if the universities trained people to apply those techniques, efficiency in government was achievable.

The study of administration was one fruit of the "revolt" of the first generation of American-trained graduate students against their German-trained teachers. The revolt, "turning the comparative method against the idealism of Burgess and Adams,"[3] was led by Goodnow at Columbia and by Wilson at Johns Hopkins. "Nothing was more central to this revolt than the emerging study of public law and administration."[4]

133

But Michael Frisch, in referring to a "revolt," cannot mean to suggest that Burgess, for example, did not regard the study of administration as essential to political science. Among the professors with whom Burgess studied at Berlin was Rudolph von Gneist who purported to show in his books and lectures how the continuity of a state over time was a function not of its constitution or legislature, but of its administrative apparatus. Moreover, in the planning of the Columbia School of Political Science, Burgess allocated one of the original four teaching positions to the subject of public administration. The revolt was on another level. Burgess adhered to a version of the doctrine of progress according to which progress was guaranteed by the working of the world spirit in time, and was therefore politically conservative. But his protégé, Goodnow, along with Woodrow Wilson and some others, accepted a different version of the doctrine of progress, according to which progress required active participation and was subject to being guided and channeled. The new science of public administration was conceived in the service of the political reform movement that shared this version of the doctrine of progress.

It cannot be too surprising that the section of the A.P.S.A. that dealt with public administration was from the beginning the most active. The original suggestion that led to the founding of the Association, the suggestion to form a society for the study of comparative legislation, actually reflected a concern with administrative practice. The founding president of the A.P.S.A. (Frank J. Goodnow) was a specialist in public administration. The concern with administration, that is, with systematizing it and making it more efficient, follows directly from the "ideology of progress" that characterized American political science in the late nineteenth and early twentieth centuries. The flow of history guaranteed the ends of politics; political science could serve those ends by becoming administrative science, by improving the means available for implementing the ends supplied externally.

The distinction between politics and administration, made, for example, by Woodrow Wilson and Frank J. Goodnow, was consistent with the theory of political progress even as advanced by Burgess and others of the German school. The Hegelian "conception of the will of the State and its expression tinged much of the thought on administration" at the end of the nineteenth century: "the distinction, between the State will and its realization in action, lay behind the whole structure of thought in this period of the development of 'public administration.'"[5] Not surprisingly, one scholar has found that conception most prevalent in the work of Frank J. Goodnow.[6]

The concern with administration was also a sign of progress, since it was an indication that America had solved its constitutional problems, and was ready to move on to more practically relevant matters. In 1891, the historian Francis N. Thorpe wrote:

> We have worked out a representative government after an apprenticeship of nearly two centuries, and in our daily administration of that form of government we are now serving an apprenticeship in administration. Whether our apprenticeship in administration shall be as long as our apprenticeship in working out the principles of government no man can tell.[7]

In this view, the American Revolution remained essentially uncompleted until the end of the Civil War. Regional differences led to a protracted debate over the constitution of the Republic and political questions were elevated to the level of a disagreement about the form of the government. The Civil War, however, in the triumph of Union arms, resolved the problem in favor of the nationalist view. But the administrative practices followed in the day-to-day business of government at all levels had been neglected in the preoccupation with great constitutional questions; the victory of nationalism opened the way to the perfection of administrative techniques adequate to the new consensus.

The students of administration, including Goodnow and Wilson, wrote as if there was a clear dichotomy between politics and administration. The current understanding of Goodnow's work is based on a particular understanding of this dichotomy: "the consensus seems to be that he offered the latter as a substitute for the former, seeking to isolate a value-free sphere of efficient government from the turmoil of politics."[8] Goodnow was originally turned to the study of administrative law by Burgess, as a part of his division of labor within the School of Political Science. But the "famous politics/administration dichotomy" was a product of his involvement with urban reform.

The American city had the anomalous status within the American legal system of a unit of government with no claim to legislative power; a series of court decisions had defined the city as a corporation wholly subject to the legislative power of the state. Goodnow offered administration as a practical way out of this "formal cul-de-sac."[9] Wilson, however, understood the dichotomy in a much larger context, and for him, "government in action—real government—was administration."[10]

A discussion of the place of the science of administration in the new American political science must focus, to a large extent, on Wilson's 1887 essay in the *Political Science Quarterly*. For, "[a]lthough Wilson himself never published most of the writings and notes on administrative law and history which fill the volumes of his collected papers for these years, such studies were his major intellectual preoccupation throughout the early 1890s."[11] Such studies, as a matter of fact were the major intellectual preoccupation not only of Wilson for a few years, but of the whole profession for most of the founding period.

Wilson asserted in the essay that although public administration was most fully developed as a science in the oligarchic states of continental Europe, it was America that had the most need for such a science, because it "is harder for democracy to organize administration than monarchy."[12] The people as rulers of the state are not as readily accessible to those with professional expertise as are kings or oligarchs. "Wherever regard for public opinion is a first principle of government, practical reform must be slow and all reform must be full of compromises."[13] Although democracy—the rule of public opinion—is the most desirable form of government, democratic politics—the shaping of public opinion—may be the greatest obstacle to reform and progress. A science of administration is the solution to that paradox.

Administration can remove the necessity of building a public consensus in favor of reform:

> The field of administration is a field of business. It is removed from the hurry and strife of politics; it at most points stands apart even from the debatable ground of constitutional study. It is a part of political life . . . only as machinery is part of the manufactured product.[14]

The most important observation to be made about administration, Wilson asserted, was "that administration lies outside the proper sphere of politics. Administrative questions are not political questions."[15] Wilson thought that politics should provide only the broadest of guidance to administrators, who would then enjoy great latitude in choosing the methods by which political goals were to be carried out. He openly declared "that large powers and unhampered discretion seem to me the indispensable conditions of responsibility."[16]

That brings him to the "fundamental problem" of how to reconcile popular sovereignty with responsible administration: "What part shall public opinion take in the conduct of administration? The right answer seems to be, that public opinion shall play the part of authoritative critic."[19] The methods of public administration were, for Wilson, things the public "has not a right to think and speak about imperatively," and a public with opinions about such things was merely "meddlesome."[18]

The proper methods of administration are neutral as to the forms of government they serve. That is why the United States was to learn from France, and especially Germany, what the most efficient methods were:

> Without comparative studies in government we cannot rid ourselves of the misconception that administration stands upon an essentially different basis in a democratic state from that on which it stands in a non-democratic state.[19]

Wilson was sure that there is "but one rule of good administration for all governments alike."[20] Even more importantly, it is not just the methods that are interchangeable, but "for all governments alike the legitimate ends of administration are the same."[21]

Frank J. Goodnow formally proclaimed the politics-administration dichotomy in 1900, in these words:

> [T]here are two distinct functions of government, and their differentiation, results in a differentiation, though less complete, of the organs of government provided by the formal governmental system. These two functions of government may for purposes of convenience be designated respectively as Politics and Administration. Politics has to do with policies or expressions of the state will. Administration has to do with the execution of these policies.[22]

Elaborating on this distinction in a later work, Goodnow echoed a favorite saying of Wilson's: "Whenever we see the government in action as opposed to deliberation or the rendering of a judicial decision, there we say is administration."[23] Goodnow had reservations about the possibility of making a clear-cut distinction between those functions, at least in the context of American politics; nevertheless, he in principle favored "creation of an administrative machine which was to be expert, impartial, and out of the reach of the political branches of the government."[24] Administration, in a complex, modern society required, said Goodnow, the "establishment, preservation, and development of [a] vast force of officers and authorities" all for the purpose of "insuring the most efficient execution of [the popular] will after it has been expressed."[25] The autonomy of administration from politics is required precisely because "political control is liable finally to produce inefficient administration."[26]

But Goodnow recognized a kind of sliding scale of appropriateness of political control. While matters properly executive might be controlled rather directly by the political system, "there is a large part of administration which is unconnected with politics . . . because it embraces fields of semi-scientific, quasi-judicial and quasi-business or commercial activity."[27] For the performance of this part of administration, Goodnow thought there should be "a force of governmental agents absolutely free from the influence of politics."[28] But, more than that, those agents should "like judges, have considerable permanence of tenure."[29] Permanence of tenure, Goodnow thought, would tend toward efficiency in the administrative process.[30]

The theme of efficiency runs throughout Goodnow's *Politics and Administration*, until, in the conclusion, it is announced that "popular government and efficient administration" are the two "chief ends of all · political systems."[31] For the securing of those ends "a reasonably centralized administrative system is necessary."[32] Goodnow offered, as a coordinate prescription, that the political parties be greatly strengthened and centralized. The result of all the strengthening and centralizing would be a new separation and balance of powers. The political power, in the hands of strong and highly centralized parties would be separated from and balanced against the administrative power, in the hands of a strong and highly centralized bureaucracy. Goodnow displayed little concern with the content of public policy. What was important was that it should reflect the popular will and that it should be efficiently administered. Apparently there was no such thing, for him, as good or bad policy, and all policies were to be administered with equal efficiency.

Politics and Administration does not offer much in the way of a science of public administration. The only standard offered for judging administration is efficiency. The only principles of administrative practice offered are centralization, security of tenure, and independence from politics. Goodnow, like Wilson, thought that America had to learn the science of administration from Europe.

At least part of the task of learning from Europe was carried forward in Goodnow's *Comparative Administrative Law*. In the preface to that work, describing his purpose, Goodnow wrote:

[T]he work was begun by first studying with considerable care books on foreign administrative law. This was necessary, owing to the complete lack of any work in the English language on administrative law as a whole, and was possible and profitable owing to the richness of the literature of foreign administrative law. After a method of treatment had thus been obtained, the attempt was made to apply it to American law. . . . For in the present stage of the study it is to foreign writers that we must look for all scientific presentations of the subject.[33]

The reason for European predominance in the field is the greater independence from political control enjoyed by the administrative organs of France and Germany especially. Therefore, on the continent of Europe, administration, the function of the executive authority, will be found to be more important than in the other countries; and it is on this account that the study of this function of administration is pursued there with greater interest.[34]

Using the European model, Goodnow described some of the elements comprised by a science of administration:

[T]he study of administration is not taken up exclusively with a consideration of the rules of administrative action; but a large part of the time devoted to this study must be given to the subject of administrative organization. . . . Administration is the function of execution; the administration is the totality of the executive and administrative authorities.[35]

Goodnow reaches administrative action in Book V of *Comparative Administrative Law*. That subject is divided into two parts: first, the direction of administrative action, that is, the services the administration performs, which is part of the content of the State will, and which therefore varies from one State to another; and, second, the methods and forms of administrative action, which "must be everywhere essentially the same."[36] Of the latter part of the subject of administrative action Goodnow undertakes to give an account, "since it is on the efficiency and adequacy" of the whole system of administrative remedies "that the real value of private rights depends."[37]

Goodnow does not proceed directly to the problems of adequacy and efficiency, but addresses them severally in the course of a taxonomy of administrative forms and methods. It is, nevertheless, possible to isolate some of the lessons to be learned about those questions. For example, the "main means" of obtaining administrative efficiency is through centralization and administrative (as opposed to judicial or legislative) control.[38] By administrative control, Goodnow means "a disciplinary power, and a power of supervision possessed by the higher administrative officers over the lower administrative officers," and that is a type of control that "exists hardly at all in the United States."[39] The problem in the United States, of course, is that the degree of control necessary to provide efficiency of administration is frustrated by federalism and decentralization.

In general, the reader is bound to be somewhat disappointed by Goodnow's analysis of administrative forms and methods. Having been told that it is on the efficiency and adequacy of these that the security and prosperity both of the individual and of the community depend, the reader has a right to expect Goodnow to prescribe for that efficiency and adequacy. It is, in a way, the practical test of the comparative method. Unfortunately, however, Goodnow contents himself for the most part with description and categorization rather than with evaluation according to the standard of efficiency. Even where he states one requirement for efficient administration, Goodnow does not detail the means of obtaining that requirement (that is, he does not go into the details of administrative control).

At least at the local level, the study of administration coincided with the practical business of administering. One example of this is found in the career of Charles E. Merriam of the University of Chicago. Merriam received his Ph.D. in political science from Columbia in 1900. Although Merriam's principal teacher was William A. Dunning, the Columbia School of Political Science was still dominated by Burgess during Merriam's years as a graduate student, and Dunning himself was a pupil of Burgess's. Like many of the Columbia graduate students at the time, Merriam spent a year in Germany attending lectures at the University of Berlin.

Merriam began teaching at Chicago in 1900. He was recognized early as an up-and-coming young member of the political science profession; and one biographer has described Merriam's status as follows:

> Merriam's reputation began to develop within that small band which, in 1903, gathered to form the [A.P.S.A.] . . . Significantly, Merriam led an elite within that group which did not have to identify itself as former historians, and whose concerns had always rested exclusively on investigations of the methods of government.[40]

Whether or not an elite, so defined, existed within either the profession or the A.P.S.A. in the first decade of the twentieth century, Merriam's position was such that he was praised by name in A. Lawrence Lowell's presidential address to the A.P.S.A. in 1909.[41] Although Merriam's doctoral dissertation dealt with the concept of sovereignty and his first book was a history of American political theory, it was certainly the case by the middle of the first decade of this century that his concerns focused almost exclusively on investigation of the methods of government.

Merriam thought that academic political science and active political life could, and should, be combined in a single career. As his biographer put it, "A career in politics and a science of politics were . . . irrevocably intertwined. One could not have one without the other."[42] Merriam became involved, shortly after his arrival in Chicago, in research in support of municipal government reform. In 1905 he became chairman of the committee on revenue and taxation of the Chicago charter convention, and later the same year headed a privately financed project for "the investigation and improvement of municipal conditions in the City of Chicago."[43]

Merriam was elected to the Chicago City Council in 1909.[44] Early in his term he got the council to create a Bureau of Efficiency.[45] Nor was Merriam alone; the business of filling in the details left out of Goodnow's books on administration was carried on by activists and reformers, and their work was reported in the political science journals. Somewhat later than the period covered in the instant work, William B. Munro published a book which sets forth (at the city government level) the means for achieving administrative efficiency in some detail.[46] Munro's book followed up, in large measure, a beginning made in Goodnow's *City Government in the United States*,[47] but Munro had the results of two decades of experimentation in municipal reform to work with.

NOTES

1. Woodrow Wilson, "The Study of Administration," *College and State: Educational, Literary and Political Papers (1875–1913)*, ed. by R. S. Baker and W. E. Dodd (New York: Harper & Brothers, Publishers, 1925), vol. I, 131.

2. Wilson, "Study of Administration," 135.

3. Michael H. Frisch, "Urban Theorists, Urban Reform, and American Political Culture in the Progressive Period," *Political Science Quarterly* 97, no. 2 (Summer 1982): 300.

4. Frisch, "Urban Theorists," 300–301.

5. M. J. C. Vile, *Constitutionalism and the Separation of Powers* (Oxford: Clarendon Press, 1967), 278.

6. Vile, *Constitutionalism*, 278–280.

7. Francis N. Thorpe, *The Story of the Constitution of the United States* (New York: The Chautaqua Press, 1891), pages 176–177.

8. Frisch, "Urban Theorists," 308.

9. Frisch, "Urban Theorists," 309.

10. Frisch, "Urban Theorists," 301.

11. Frisch, "Urban Theorists," 302.

12 Wilson, "Study of Administration," 141.

13. Wilson, "Study of Administration," 142–143.

14. Wilson, "Study of Administration," 144.

15. Wilson, "Study of Administration," 145.

16. Wilson, "Study of Administration," 148.

17. Wilson, "Study of Administration," 149.

18. Wilson, "Study of Administration," 150.

19. Wilson, "Study of Administration," 153.

20. Wilson, "Study of Administration," 153–154.

21. Wilson, "Study of Administration," 154.

22. Goodnow, *Politics and Administration: A Study in Government* (New York: Russell & Russell, 1967), 18.

23. Goodnow, *Selections from Comparative Administrative Law*, ed. by Richard M. Pious (Farmingdale, N.Y.: Dabor Social Science Publications, 1978), 2. [Originally published in 1893.]

24. Vile, *Constitutionalism*, 280.

25. Goodnow, *Politics and Administration*, 77.

26. Goodnow, *Politics and Administration*, 82.

27. Goodnow, *Politics and Administration*, 85.

28. Goodnow, *Politics and Administration*, 85.

29. Goodnow, *Politics and Administration*, 87.

30. Goodnow, *Politics and Administration*, 91.

31. Goodnow, *Politics and Administration*, 255

32. Goodnow, *Politics and Administration*, 258.

33. Goodnow, *Comparative Administrative Law*, v.

34. Goodnow, *Comparative Administrative Law*, 37.

35. Goodnow, *Comparative Administrative Law*, 5.

36. Goodnow, *Comparative Administrative Law*, 102–103.

37. Goodnow, *Comparative Administrative Law*, 105.

38. Goodnow, *Comparative Administrative Law*, 141.

39. Goodnow, *Comparative Administrative Law*, 141.

40. Barry D. Karl, *Charles E. Merriam and the Study of Politics* (Chicago: University of Chicago Press, 1974), 50.

41. A. Lawrence Lowell, "The Physiology of Politics," *American Political Science Review* 4 (1910): 5.

42. Karl, *Charles E. Merriam*, 40.

43. Karl, *Charles E. Merriam*, 50–51.

44. Karl, *Charles E. Merriam*, 61.

45. Karl, *Charles E. Merriam*, 62.

46. William B. Munro, *Municipal Government and Administration*, 2 vols. (New York: The Macmillan Company, 1923).

47. Frank J. Goodnow, *City Government in the United States* (New York: The Century Co., 1904).

CONCLUSION

Between 1880 and the First World War, a new American political science was brought into being. That political science was, in the first instance, a translation into American terms of the *Staatswissenschaft* practiced in the German universities. The German science of politics was based upon an *allgemeine Staatslehre*, or general State theory, according to which the State was understood as an organic unity, the product of an evolutionary process. In its American version, this general State theory saw the modern democratic nation-state as the culmination of a long history of continuous and inescapable progress.

But at least two native American phenomena also greatly influenced the new political science. The first was pragmatism, a school of philosophy that emphasized the utility of information and of theories rather than their correspondence to objective reality. Pragmatism also promoted the scientific method as a means of guaranteeing progress in knowing.

The founding generation of the new American political science was composed not only of students of politics but of active participants in the political process. The emergence of the new discipline corresponded roughly with the Progressive Era, and the popular movement for political reform provided an agenda and an opportunity for the new political science. Many of the practitioners and professors of the new science participated actively in the reform movement. In any case, the reform movement provided a kind of laboratory for testing hypotheses about politics and an opportunity to practice those administrative techniques that the new political science found or hoped to find.

But the new American political science did not make its entrance onto an empty stage. There existed an American political tradition, informed by political philosophy. The American regime, and the traditional American political science, took shape from the Declaration of Independence. The Declaration asserted that the ends of government are to be found in nature and that nature is, therefore, capable of providing a standard against which political action can be measured.

In particular, the Declaration of Independence is based upon the notion of a prepolitical state of nature in which men are equally possessed of certain natural rights. In the state of nature, enjoyment of those rights is not secure; the institution of civil society, and of government, can provide security for the enjoyment of natural rights. But the institution of government can be accomplished only by the consent of those who are to be governed. Without consent, no government can justly exercise dominion over the individual.

The new American political science, however, denied the validity of analysis based on natural law or natural rights. An inquiry into the actual history of actual states was held to show that no state of nature ever existed. Instead, the State possessed, and the government exercised, inherent sovereign power. History, not nature, defined the ends of government, and then only for particular governments.

The traditional American political science was also reflected in the Constitution of the United States. In the Constitution, the Framers had attempted to provide security for the liberty of the citizens by dividing and separating the powers of government. Acknowledging that recurrence to the people is the principal check upon government in a democratic society, they nevertheless instituted auxiliary precautions, checking power with power and ambition with ambition. The expressed aim was to make the government energetic enough to protect the citizens while preventing it from becoming a threat to their freedom.

The new American political science regarded most of the auxiliary precautions of the Constitution as unwarranted and outmoded. The real division was held not to be among legislative, executive, and judicial powers, but between politics and administration. In the interest of democracy and of efficiency, the government should be so structured as to permit the majority will to assert itself in general terms and to leave a professional civil service, or administrative cadre, to formulate the details of public policy.

Certain aspects became characteristic of the new discipline. First, in accordance with pragmatist epistemology, the new political science constituted itself as an organized body of collective inquiry and action. The American Political Science Association became the official custodian of political science. Under the auspices of the A.P.S.A., political science took on the trappings of modern professional scholarship.

Second, the long quest for the appropriate methodology began. The example of modern natural science showed that progress could be guaranteed by the application of the proper method. Burgess had introduced the German historical method, but that was soon rejected because it concentrated on formal constitutions and institutional arrangements to the exclusion of the real workings of politics. In its place, Wilson and Lowell sought to introduce a descriptive method analogous to physiology. Finally, toward the close of the period under study, a group of political scientists proposed to redefine the subject matter of politics in ways that would permit quantification.

But throughout the founding period, and despite differences concerning methodology, the new political scientists tried to prove that theirs was a useful science. There was general agreement that the efficiency of government could be enhanced by improvements in administration. Therefore, an attempt was made to develop a science of administration, that is to develop techniques themselves politically neutral for the efficient execution of whatever aims might be determined in the political process.

The First World War, in which the most progressive nation-states engaged in the most brutal combat against one another, badly shook the discipline of political science. The historical-comparative school was devastated by the war, and the quantitative measurement school emerged dominant. Arthur F. Bentley was still active, of course; then Charles E. Merriam published *New Aspects of Politics* and turned to the methods of sociology. Harold Laswell, a young member of Merriam's department at the University of Chicago, tried to redefine political science as merely the study of who gets what and how.

The history of American political science since the First World War spans eighty-five years, and yet the same themes are significant now as at the end of the founding era: organization, methodology, administration. In a sense we are still living in the Progressive Era, except that the doctrine of inevitable progress, which, in one form or another, influenced and gave impetus to the creation of modern political science, is no longer viable to justify its continuation. The result is a discipline that is adrift, that can quote numbers forever but that has lost touch with the political things.

The differences between the political science of the Progressive Era and that of the last quarter of the twentieth century are many and striking, but they do not go to the essentials of the discipline. The discipline still affects to engage in dispassionate scientific study of those matters about which human beings, in their public lives, care most passionately. Inevitably, there is a tension between the results of the scientific study of politics and the political sentiments of the scientists, which leads to what has been aptly termed the "tragedy of political science."[1]

Nothing in the history of the period from the First World War I to the present so reveals the crisis in American political science as the discipline's treatment of the phenomenon of totalitarianism. The two great revolutions of the interwar period gave rise to the dictatorship of the Bolsheviks in Russia and of the National Socialists in Germany. Nothing in political science as it was taught and practiced in America provided or recognized a standard against which these acts of national self-determination and these expressions of the state will in their respective societies could be tried and found wanting. Indeed, to some political scientists, the first of these phenomena appeared as the leading edge of the continuing process of political evolution.

Thus, on the question of political legitimacy, the question of constitutional government versus tyranny, political science was tragically silent. A political science which recognizes better and worse only in the form of new and old is at a loss to explain new conditions that are evidently worse than what they replaced.

But political science has also been tragically outspoken on another great regime question, namely the rise of bureaucracy and the substitution of administration for politics. The study of administration and the quest for efficiency of administration were, of course, characteristics of the emerging discipline. The leaders of the discipline were active participants in the rise of the administrative state. As John Marini has pointed out, the administrative state "has remained a contentious issue in American politics and has lacked legitimacy because it rests upon a theory of government that is outside the American political tradition."[2] As Marini notes, the "theory upon which the administrative state is based . . . developed as a practical outgrowth of German idealist philosophy" of the late nineteenth and early twentieth centuries and "stands in sharp contrast to the government created by a limited Constitution."[3]

Indeed, academic American political science continues to be at odds, as it was at its emergence, with the old political science represented by the Declaration of Independence and the Constitution of the United States. As Marini has pointed out, Progressives, prominently including political scientist Woodrow Wilson, "insisted that the real source of power in the modern state lies in the administrative realm: in the practical operation of the bureaucracy," and, consequently, the "distinction between politics and administration was to replace the fundamental distinction [among] the powers of government."[4] And administration is not peculiar to constitutional or republican government, but is "within the domain of those universal things commonly associated with science."[5] The transformation that was espoused by political scientists in the Progressive Era has now succeeded to the extent that it has undermined the very foundations of what was once an American political tradition.

If the emphasis on administration, especially the empirical study of administrative methods with a view toward increasing efficiency, brought the new political science into conflict with the old political science upon which American institutions were established, another aspect of the discipline may be seen to have moved it in the opposite direction. The emphasis on scientific methods, and the quest for a distinctive methodology, led to rise of the vapid and irrelevant "behavioralist" school, which dominated academic political science in the third quarter of the twentieth century.

Bernard Crick has called research an "ideal" of the "democratic gospel," and wrote that Charles E. Merriam was "far from alone in this faith" that further research was the solution to social problems.[6] In pursuit of this "faith," American political science by the end of the 1920s found itself "under some compulsion to show that it could be as scientific, as research-conscious, as sociology or as a 'unified social science' would be."[7] By the 1930s, Harold Laswell and T. V. Smith publicly stated the view that the claim to scientific rigor was "more important than the specific content of any research."[8] Even the fundamental rationale for scientific research about politics changed unselfconsciously: pragmatism "changed into positivism without many noticing the difference."[9]

But Laswell, like Merriam before him, was a political reformer who still envisioned a political science in the service of reform. The behavioral revolution after the Second World War was based to some extent not only on the negation of the notion of science in the public service but on an assertion of the incompatibility of science with public service. "Rather than envisioning a political role for the discipline . . . behavioralists sought to transform political science into a pure science of the political process."[10] They distinguished scientific inquiry from all other forms of intellectual activity, and "the key to this dichotomy was the distinction between the realm of what is and the realm of what ought to be."[11] Even at the end of the twentieth century the dichotomy persists: when "political scientists try to answer the question of how we are governed, they . . . claim to study *facts*, not *values*."[12]

The development after the First World War of two of the characteristics of American political science in its founding generation, the emphasis on administration and the quest for scientific validity, may appear to tend in opposite directions. But this is not necessarily the case. Theodore Lowi, who was himself the president of the A.P.S.A. in the early 1990s, has offered his "political analysis" that the hegemony of behavioralism over the discipline in the later twentieth century "was to a large extent a product of its compatibility with bureaucratic thought-ways, rather than the result of a successful discourse within political science."[13] The notion of a nonpolitical science of politics was a result of self-delusion; the new science was, perhaps unwittingly, simply science in the service of the administrative state.

American political science at the beginning of the twenty-first century, a hundred years after the founding of the A.P.S.A., is still under the powerful influence of its own founding era. It is especially, although this is not often acknowledged, under the influence of the doctrine of progress, introduced by various routes from nineteenth-century German idealist philosophy. In a sense, American political science as a discipline remains foreign to the American regime, and therefore incapable either of understanding or explaining that regime.

What was wanting in 1903 remains wanting a century later, and that is an academic political science rooted in the self-evident truths upon which the American republic was founded. That requires, in the first instance, a political science that takes seriously the possibility of truth: not just contingent truth about what is, but of permanent and transcendent truth about what ought to be. That, in turn, requires a revival of political philsophy, as the serious inquiry into natural right. Upon a revived political philosophy could be built a political science capable of confonting the crisis of the American regime, which is also the crisis of civilization.

NOTES

1. David M. Ricci, *The Tragedy of Political Science: Politics, Scholarship, and Democracy* (New Haven, Conn.: Yale University Press, 1984).

2. John Marini, *The Politics of Budget Control: Congress, the Presidency, and the Growth of the Administrative State* (Washington, D.C.: Crane Russak, 1992), 184.

3. Marini, *Politics of Budget Control*, 2–3.

4. John A. Marini, "Introduction," in *The Imperial Congress: Crisis in the Separation of Powers* ed. by Gordon S. Jones and John A. Marini (New York: Pharos Books, 1988), 17.

5. Marini, *Politics of Budget Control*, 46.

6. Bernard Crick, *The American Science of Politics: Its Origins and Conditions* (Berkeley: University of California Press, 1964), 156.

7. Crick, *American Science*, 156.

8. Crick, *American Science*, 171.

9. Crick, *American Science*, 175.

10. Raymond Seidelman, *Disenchanted Realists: Political Science and the American Crisis, 1884–1994* (Albany: State University of New York Press, 1985), 150.

11. Ricci, *Tragedy*, 136–137.

12. Thomas G. West, "The Constitutionalism of the Founders versus Modern Liberalism," *Nexus*, 6 (2001): 76.

13. Theodore Lowi, "The State in Political Science: How We Became What We Study," in *Public Philosophy and Political Science* ed. by E. Robert Statham Jr. (Lanham, Md.: Lexington Books, 2002).

BIBLIOGRAPHY

Adams, James T. *Epic of America*. Boston: Little, Brown, and Company 1931.

Baker, Roy S. *Woodrow Wilson: Life and Letters*, volume 1, *Youth: 1856–1890*; volume 2, *Princeton: 1890–1910*. Garden City, N.Y.: Doubleday, Page & Co. 1927.

Barnes, Harry E., ed. *The History and Prospects of the Social Sciences*. New York: Alfred A. Knopf, 1925.

Barrett, William. *The Illusion of Technique*. New York: Doubleday (Anchor), 1978.

Beard, Charles A. *The Economic Basis of Politics and Related Writings*, ed. by William Beard. New York: Vintage Books, 1957.

——————. *An Economic Interpretation of the Constitution of the United States*. New York: The Macmillan Company, 1935.

Bentley, Arthur F. *The Process of Government: A Study in Social Pressures*. Chicago: University of Chicago Press, 1908. [Reprinted, Cambridge, Mass.: Belknap Press of Harvard University Press, 1967.]

Bergner, Jeffrey T. *The Origin of Formalism in Social Science*. Chicago: University of Chicago Press, 1981.

Bledstein, Burton J. *The Culture of Professionalism: The Middle Class and the Development of Higher Education in America*. New York: W.W. Norton & Company, Inc., 1976.

Blum, John M. *The Republican Roosevelt*. New York: Atheneum, 1962. [Originally published by Harvard University Press, 1954.]

——————. *Woodrow Wilson and the Politics of Morality*. Boston: Little, Brown, and Company, 1956.

Bluntschli, Johann K. *The Theory of the State* (translated from the sixth German edition by D. G. Ritchie, P. E. Matheson, and R. Lodge). Oxford: The Clarendon Press, 1885.

153

Boller, Paul F., Jr. *American Thought in Transition: The Impact of Evolutionary Naturalism, 1865–1900*. Chicago: Rand McNally & Company, 1969. (Rand McNally Series on the History of American Thought and Culture.)

Bragdon, Henry W. *Woodrow Wilson: The Academic Years*. Cambridge, Mass.: The Belknap Press of Harvard University Press, 1967.

Braybrooke, David, ed. *Philosophical Problems of the Social Sciences*. New York: The Macmillan Company, 1965.

Brown, Bernard E. *American Conservatives: The Political Thought of Francis Lieber and John W. Burgess*. New York: Columbia University Press, 1951.

Bryce, James. "The Relations of Political Science to History and to Practice." *The American Political Science Review*, vol. 3 (1909), 1–19.

Burgess, John W. *Political Science and Comparative Constitutional Law* (2 volumes). Boston: Ginn & Company, 1890.

————. *Recent Changes in American Constitutional Theory*. New York: Columbia University Press, 1923.

————. *The Reconciliation of Government with Liberty*. New York: Charles Scribner's Sons, 1915.

————. *Reminiscences of an American Scholar: The Beginnings of Columbia University*. Morningside Heights, N.Y.: Columbia University Press, 1934.

Bury, J. B. *The Idea of Progress: An Inquiry into Its Origin and Growth*. New York: Dover Publications, Inc., 1932.

Chamberlain, John. *Farewell to Reform: Being a History of the Rise, Life, and Decay of the Progressive Mind in America*. New York: Liveright, Inc., 1932.

Cohen, Stanley, ed. *Reform, War, and Reaction: 1912–1932*. New York: Harper & Row, Publishers, 1972. (Documentary History of the United States series.)

Coker, Francis W. *Recent Political Thought*. New York: D. Appleton-Century Company, 1934.

Collini, Stefan, Donald Winch, and John Burrow. *That Noble Science of Politics: A Study in Nineteenth-Century Intellectual History*. Cambridge: Cambridge University Press, 1983.

Commager, Henry Steele. *The American Mind: An Interpretation of American Thought and Character since the 1880's*. New Haven, Conn.: Yale University Press, 1950.

Crick, Bernard. *In Defense of Politics*, revised edition. Harmondsworth, Middlesex, England: Penguin Books Ltd., 1964. [First edition published in 1962.]

————. *The American Science of Politics: Its Origin and Conditions*. Berkeley and Los Angeles: University of California Press, 1959.

Croly, Herbert. *Progressive Democracy*. New York: The Macmillan Company, 1914.

————. *The Promise of American Life*. Indianapolis, Ind.: The Bobbs-Merrill Company, Inc., 1965. (American Heritage Series.) [Originally published in 1909.]

Davis, W. H. Carless. *The Political Thought of Heinrich von Treitschke*. New York: Charles Scribner's Sons 1915.

De Witt, Benjamin P. *The Progressive Movement: A Nonpartisan, Comprehensive Discussion of Current Tendencies in American Politics*. New York: The Macmillan Company, 1915.

Dewey, John. *German Philosophy and Politics*. Freeport, N.Y.: Books for Libraries Press, 1970. [Originally published in 1915].

————. *How We Think: A Restatement of the Relation of Reflective Thinking to the Educative Process*. Boston: D.C. Heath and Company, 1933.

——————. *Reconstruction in Philosophy*. New York: New American Library, 1950. [Originally published, 1920.]

Dupree, A. Hunter, ed. *Science and the Emergence of Modern America, 1865–1916*. Chicago: Rand McNally & Company, 1963.

Easton, David. *The Political System: An Inquiry into the State of Political Science*, 2d edition. New York: Alfred A. Knopf, 1971. [First edition published in 1953.]

Elliott, W. Y. *The Pragmatic Revolt in Politics: Syndicalism, Fascism, and the Constitutional State*. New York: The Macmillan Company, 1928.

Emerson, Rupert. *State and Sovereignty in Modern Germany*. New Haven, Conn.: Yale University Press, 1928.

Flower, B. O. *Progressive Men, Women, and Movements of the Past Twenty-Five Years*. Boston: The New Arena, 1914.

Forcey, Charles. *The Crossroads of Liberalism: Croly, Weyl, Lippmann and the Progressive Era, 1900–1925*. New York: Oxford University Press, 1961.

Ford, Henry Jones. *The Natural History of the State: An Introduction to Political Science*. Princeton, N.J.: Princeton University Press, 1915.

——————. "Present Tendencies in American Politics." *The American Political Science Review*, vol. 14 (1920): 1–13.

——————. *Representative Government*. New York: Henry Holt and Company, 1924.

——————. "The Scope of Political Science." *Proceedings of the American Political Science Association*, vol. 2 (1905): 198–206.

Frederickson, George M. *The Inner Civil War: Northern Intellectuals and the Crisis of the Union*. New York: Harper & Row, Publishers, 1965.

Garner, James W. *Introduction to Political Science: A Treatise on the Origin, Nature, Functions, and Organization of the State*. New York: American Book Company, 1910.

Gettell, Raymond G. *An Introduction to Political Science*. Boston: Ginn and Company, 1910.

——————. *Problems in Political Evolution*. Boston: Ginn and Company, 1913.

Gneist, Rudolph von. *The History of the English Constitution* (translated from the German by Philip A. Ashworth.). London: William Clowes and Sons, Limited, 1891.

——————. *History of the English Parliament: Its Growth and Development* (translated from the fourth German edition by A. H. Keane). London: William Clowes and Sons, Limited, 1895.

Goldman, Eric F. *Rendezvous with Destiny: A History of Modern American Reform*, revised edition. New York: Vintage Books, 1955.

Goodnow, Frank J. *City Government in the United States*. New York: The Century Co., 1904.

——————. *Politics and Administration: A Study in Government*. New York: Russell & Russell, 1967. [Originally published in 1900.]

——————. *Selections from Comparative Administrative Law*, ed. by Richard M. Pious. Farmingdale. N.Y.: Dabor Social Science Publications, 1978. [Originally published in 1893.]

——————. *Social Reform and the Constitution*. New York: The Macmillan Company, 1911.

——————. "The Work of the American Political Science Association." *Proceedings of the American Political Science Association*, vol. 1 (1904): 35–46.

Greene, John C. *Darwin and the Modern World View*. New York: New American Library, 1963.

John G. Gunnell. *The Descent of Political Theory: The Genealogy of an American Vocation*. Chicago: University of Chicago Press, 1983.

——————. *Political Theory: Tradition and Interpretation*. Lanham, Md.: University Press of America, 1987.

Hacker, Andrew. *The Study of Politics: The Western Tradition and American Origins*. New York: McGraw-Hill Book Company, Inc., 1963. (Foundations of American Government and Political Science series.)

Haddow, Anna. *Political Science in American Colleges and Universities, 1636–1900*. New York and London: D. Appleton-Century Company, Incorporated, 1939.

Haines, Charles G., and Marshall E. Dimock, eds. *Essays on the Law and Practice of Governmental Administration*. Baltimore: The Johns Hopkins Press, 1935.

Hartz, Louis. *The Liberal Tradition in America: An Interpretation of American Political Thought since the Revolution*. New York: Harcourt, Brace & World, Inc., 1955.

Haskell, Thomas L. *The Emergence of Professional Social Science: The American Social Science Association and the Nineteenth-Century Crisis of Authority*. Urbana, Ill.: University of Illinois Press, 1977.

Hausrath, Adolf. *Treitschke: His Doctrine of German Destiny and of International Relations* (translated from the German). New York and London: G.P. Putnam's Sons, 1914.

Hays, Samuel P. *The Response to Industrialism, 1885–1914*. Chicago: University of Chicago Press, 1957.

Herbst, Jurgen. *The German Historical School in American Scholarship: A Study in the Transfer of Culture*. Ithaca, N.Y.: Cornell University Press, 1965.

Hofstadter, Richard. *The Age of Reform: From Bryan to F.D.R.* New York: Vintage Books, 1955.

——————. *The American Political Tradition and the Men who Made It*. New York: Vantage Books, 1948.

——————. *The Progressive Historians: Turner, Beard, Parrington*. Chicago, Ill.: The University of Chicago Press, 1979. [Originally published, New York: Alfred E. Knopf, Inc., 1968.]

——————, ed. *The Progressive Movement: 1900–1915*. Englewood Cliffs, N.J.: Prentice-Hall, Inc., 1963.

——————. *Social Darwinism in American Thought*, revised edition. Boston: The Beacon Press, 1955. [Original edition published by the University of Pennsylvania Press in 1944.]

Hofstadter, Richard, and C. DeWitt Hardy. *The Development and Scope of Higher Education in the United States*. New York and London: Columbia University Press, 1952.

Hruska, Thomas J. *Woodrow Wilson: The Organic State and His Political Theory*. Unpublished Ph.D. dissertation, Claremont Graduate School, 1978.

Hugh-Jones, E. M. *Woodrow Wilson and American Liberalism*. New York: Collier Books, 1962. (Originally published by The Macmillan Company, 1947.)

Jaffa, Harry V. *American Conservatism and the American Founding*. Durham, N.C.: Carolina Academic Press, 1984.

——————. *Crisis of the House Divided: An Interpretation of the Lincoln-Douglas Debates*. Garden City, N.Y.: Doubleday & Company, Inc., 1959.

——————. *Equality and Liberty: Theory and Practice in American Politics*. New York: Oxford University Press, 1965.

——————. *A New Birth of Freedom: Abraham Lincoln and the Coming of the Civil War*. Lanham, Md.: Rowman & Littlefield Publishers, Inc., 2000.

James, William. *Essays in Pragmatism*, ed. by Alburey Castell. New York: Hafner Publishing Company, 1966.

——————. *The Meaning of Truth: A Sequel to Pragmatism*. Ann Arbor, Mich.: The University of Michigan Press, 1970. [Originally published in 1909.]

——————. *Pragmatism*. Cleveland, Ohio: The World Publishing Company, 1955. [Originally published in 1907.]

——————. *Selected Letters*, ed. by Elizabeth Hardwick. Boston: David R. Godine, Publisher, 1980.

Joad, C. E. M. *Guide to Philosophy*. London: Victor Gollancz, Ltd., 1941.

Karl, Barry D. *Charles E. Merriam and the Study of Politics*. Chicago: University of Chicago Press, 1974.

Lewis, Edward R. *A History of American Political Thought: From the Civil War to the World War*. New York: The Macmillan Company, 1937.

Link, Arthur S. *The American Epoch: A History of the United States since the 1890's*, 2d edition. New York: Alfred A. Knopf, 1963. [First edition published in 1955.]

Lippmann, Walter. *A Preface to Morals*. New York: The Macmillan Company, 1929.

——————. *A Preface to Politics*. Ann Arbor, Mich.: The University of Michigan Press, 1962. [Originally published in 1914.]

Loewenberg, Bert James. "John W. Burgess, the Scientific Method, and the Hegelian Philosophy of History." *Mississippi Valley Historical Review*, vol. 42 (1955): 490–509.

Lowell, A. Lawrence. "The Physiology of Politics." *The American Political Science Review*, vol. 4 (1910): 5–15.

Mackenzie, W. J. M. *Politics and Social Science*. Baltimore, Md.: Penguin Books, 1967.

Marini, John. *The Politics of Budget Control: Congress, the Presidency, and the Growth of the Administrative State*. Washington, D.C.: Crane-Russak, 1992.

Marnell, William H. *Man-Made Morals: Four Philosophies That Shaped America*. Garden City, N.Y.: Doubleday & Company, Inc., 1966.

Mathews, John Mabry, and James Hart, eds. *Essays in Political Science in Honor of Westel Woodbury Willoughby*. Baltimore, Md.: The Johns Hopkins Press, 1937.

May, Henry F. *The End of American Innocence: A Study of the First Years of Our Own Times, 1912–1917*. New York: Alfred A. Knopf, 1959.

McDonald, Forrest. *The United States in the Twentieth Century*, volume 1, *1900–1920*. Reading, Mass., and Menlo Park, Calif.: Addison-Wesley Publishing Company 1970.

Merriam, Charles E. *American Political Ideas: Studies in the Development of American Political Thought, 1865–1917*. New York: The Macmillan Company, 1920.

——————. *A History of American Political Theories*. New York: The Macmillan Company, 1920.

——————. *New Aspects of Politics*. Chicago: University of Chicago Press, 1925.

——————. "Recent Advances in Political Methods." *The American Political Science Review*, vol. 17 (1923): 275–295.

——————. *The Role of Politics in Social Change*. New York: New York University Press, 1936.

Meyer, Adolph E. *An Educational History of the American People.* New York: McGraw-Hill Book Company, Inc., 1957.

Mowry, George E. *The California Progressives.* Chicago: Quadrangle Books, 1963. [Originally published Berkeley: University of California Press, 1951.]

Munro, William B. *The Government of the United States: National, State, and Local,* 3d edition. New York: The Macmillan Company 1933. [First edition published in 1919.]

————. *The Makers of the Unwritten Constitution.* New York: The Macmillan Company, 1930.

————. *Municipal Government and Administration.* New York: The Macmillan Company, 1923.

Nisbet, Robert. *History of the Idea of Progress.* New York: Basic Books, Inc., 1980.

Noble, David W. *The Progressive Mind, 1890–1917.* Chicago: Rand McNally & Company, 1970. (Rand McNally Series on the History of American Thought and Culture.)

Nye, Russel B. *Midwestern Progressive Politics: A Historical Study of Its Origins and Development, 1870–1958.* New York: Harper & Row, Publishers, 1959.

Oleson, Alexandra, and Sanborn C. Brown, eds. *The Pursuit of Knowledge in the Early American Republic: Scientific and Learned Societies form Colonial Times to the Civil War.* Baltimore, Md.: The Johns Hopkins University Press, 1976.

O'Neill, William L. *The Progressive Years: America Comes of Age.* New York: Dodd, Mead & Company, 1975.

Parrington, Vernon L. *Main Currents in American Thought,* volume 3, *The Beginnings of Critical Realism in America, 1860–1920.* New York: Harcourt, Brace & World, Inc., 1930.

Peirce, Charles S. *Philosophical Writings,* selected and edited by Justus Blucher. New York: Dover Publications, Inc., 1955. [This edition first published London: 1940; individual essays originally published 1868–1905.]

Pollock, James K., et al. *The Status and Prospects of Political Science as a Discipline.* Ann Arbor, Mich.: The University of Michigan Department of Political Science, 1960.

Popper, Karl R. *The Poverty of Historicism.* New York and Evanston, Ill.: Harper & Row, Publishers, 1964. [Originally published in 1957.]

Ranney, Austin, ed. *Essays on the Behavioral Study of Politics.* Urbana, Ill.: University of Illinois Press, 1962.

Ricci, David M. *The Tragedy of Political Science: Politics, Scholarship, and Democracy.* New Haven, Conn.: Yale University Press, 1984.

Riley, Woodbridge. *American Thought: From Puritanism to Pragmatism.* New York: Henry Holt and Company, 1915.

Ringer, Fritz K. *The Decline of the German Mandarins: The German Academic Community, 1890–1933.* Cambridge, Mass.: Harvard University Press, 1969.

Robinson, Daniel Sommer, ed. *An Anthology of Recent Philosophy.* New York: Thomas Y. Crowell Company, Publishers, 1929.

Ross, Dorothy. "Socialism and American Liberalism: Academic Social Thought in the 1880's." *Perspectives in American History,* vol. 11 (1977): 7–79.

Sabine, George H. "The Pragmatic Approach to Politics." *The American Political Science Review,* vol. 24 (1930): 865–885.

Schlesinger, Arthur M. *The American as Reformer.* New York: Atheneum, 1968. [Originally published by Harvard University Press in 1950.]

Schramm, Peter W., and Bradford P. Wilson, eds. *American Political Parties and Constitutional Politics*. Lanham, Md.: Rowman & Littlefield Publishers, Inc., 1993.

Seidelman, Raymond, and Edward J. Harpham. *Disenchanted Realists: Political Science and the American Crisis, 1884–1984*. Albany, N.Y.: State University of New York Press, 1985.

Shannon, David A., ed. *Progressivism and Postwar Disillusionment: 1898–1928*. New York: McGraw-Hill Book Company, 1966.

Shaw, Albert. "Presidential Address." *The American Political Science Review*, vol. 1 (1907): 177–186.

Silver, Thomas B. *Coolidge and the Historians*. Durham, N.C.: Carolina Academic Press, 1983.

Smith, J. Allen. *The Spirit of American Government: A Study of the Constitution: Its Origin, Influence and Relation to Democracy*. New York: The Macmillan Company, 1919.

Smith, Monroe. "The Domain of Political Science." *Political Science Quarterly*, vol. 1 (1886): 1–8.

Somit, Albert, and Joseph Tannenhaus. *American Political Science: A Profile of a Discipline*. New York: Atherton Press, 1964.

——————. *The Development of American Political Science from Burgess to Behavioralism*. Boston: Allyn and Bacon, Inc., 1967.

Storing, Herbert J., ed. *Essays on the Scientific Study of Politics*. New York: Holt, Rinehart and Winston, Inc., 1962.

Stratham, E. Robert, Jr., ed. *Public Philosophy and Political Science: Crisis and Reflection*. Lanham, Md.: Lexington Books, 2002.

Strauss, Leo. *Natural Right and History*. Chicago: University of Chicago Press, 1950.

——————. *What Is Political Philosophy? and Other Studies*. New York: The Free Press, 1959.

Thorpe, Francis N. *The Story of the Constitution of the United States*. New York: Chautauqua Press, 1891.

Treitschke, Heinrich von. *History of Germany in the Nineteenth Century*, translated by Eden and Cedar Paul; abridged and edited by Gordon A. Craig. Chicago: University of Chicago Press, 1975. [Original German edition published in five volumes, Berlin, 1879–1894; translation originally published in seven volumes, London, 1914–1919.]

——————. *Politics*, translated from the German by Blanche Dugdale and Torben de Bille; abridged and edited by Hans Kohn. New York and Burlingame, Calif.: Harcourt, Brace & World, Inc. 1963. [Abridged from the two-volume edition published London, 1916.]

Veblen, Thorstein. *The Higher Learning in America: A Memorandum on the Conduct of Universities by Business Men*. New York: Sagamore Press Inc., 1957. [Originally published in 1918.]

Veysey, Laurence R. *The Emergence of the American University*. Chicago and London: University of Chicago Press, 1965.

Vile, M. J. C. *Constitutionalism and the Separation of Powers*. Oxford: The Clarendon Press, 1967.

Voegelin, Eric. *The New Science of Politics: An Introduction*. Chicago: The University of Chicago Press, 1952.

Waldo, Dwight. *The Administrative State: A Study in the Political Theory of American Public Administration*. New York: The Ronald Press Company, 1948.

Wasby, Stephen L. *Political Science—The Discipline and Its Dimensions: An Introduction.* New York: Charles Scribner's Sons, 1970.

Weyl, Walter E. *The New Democracy: An Essay on Certain Political and Economic Tendencies in the United States.* New York: Harper & Row, Publishers, 1964. [Originally published in 1912.]

White, Andrew D. *European Schools of History and Politics.* Baltimore, Md.: Johns Hopkins University, 1887.

————. *Autobiography.* New York: The Century Company, 1907.

————. *Education in Political Science.* Baltimore: Johns Hopkins University Press, 1880.

White, Morton G. *The Origin of Dewey's Instrumentalism.* New York: Octagon Books, 1964.

————. *Pragmatism and the American Mind: Essays and Reviews in Philosophy and Intellectual History.* New York: Oxford University Press, 1973.

————. *Science and Sentiment in America: Philosophical Thought from Jonathan Edwards to John Dewey.* New York: Oxford University Press, 1972.

————. *Social Thought in America: The Revolt against Formalism.* Boston: Beacon Press, 1957. [Republished, with new preface and epilogue, from edition of 1949.]

Wiebe, Robert H. *The Search for Order: 1877–1920.* New York: Hill and Wang, 1967. (American Century Series: The Making of America.)

Willoughby, Westel W. *The American Constitutional System: An Introduction to the Study of the American State.* New York: The Century Co., 1904. [Reprinted, Farmingdale, N.Y.: Dabor Social Science Publications, 1978.]

————. *An Examination of the Nature of the State: A Study in Political Philosophy.* New York: Macmillan and Co., 1896. [Reprinted, Farmingdale, N.Y.: Dabor Social Science Publications, 1978.]

————. "The Political Theories of John W. Burgess." *Yale Review*, vol. 17 (1909): 59–84.

————. *Prussian Political Philosophy: Its Principles and Implications.* New York and London: D. Appleton and Company, 1918.

————. *Social Justice: A Critical Essay.* New York: The Macmillan Company 1900.

————. "The Value of Political Philosophy." *Political Science Quarterly*, vol. 15 (1900): 75–95.

Willoughby, Westel W., and Lindsay Rogers. *An Introduction to the Problem of Government.* Garden City, N.Y.: Doubleday, Page & Co., 1922.

Wilson, R. Jackson, ed. *Reform, Crisis, and Confusion, 1900–1929.* New York: Random House, 1970. (Volume 5 in the Readings in American History Series.)

Wilson, Woodrow. *College and State: Educational, Literary and Political Papers (1875–1913),* ed. by Roy S. Baker and William E. Dodd). New York and London: Harper & Brothers Publishers 1925.

————. *Congressional Government: A Study in American Politics.* New York: Meridian Books, Inc., 1956. [Originally published in 1885.]

————. *Constitutional Government in the United States.* New York: Columbia University Press, 1908.

————. *George Washington.* New York: Schocken Books, 1969. [Originally published in 1896.]

_____. *A History of the American People.* 5 volumes. New York: Harper & Brothers, Publishers, 1902.

_____. "The Law and the Facts." *The American Political Science Review*, vol. 5 (1911): 1–11.

_____. *The New Freedom: A Call for the Emancipation of the Generous Energies of a People.* Englewood Cliffs, N.J.: Prentice-Hall, Inc., 1961. [Originally published in 1913.]

_____. *The State: Elements of Historical and Practical Politics.* Boston: D.C. Heath & Co., Publishers 1897. [Originally published in 1889.]

Wiseman, Victor. *Politics: The Master Science: An Introduction to Politics as a Practical Art and an Academic Discipline.* New York: Pegasus, 1969.

Young, Oran R. *Systems of Political Science.* Englewood Cliffs, N.J.: Prentice-Hall, Inc. 1968.

Zvesper, John. *Political Philosophy and Rhetoric: A Study of the Origins of American Party Politics.* Cambridge: Cambridge University Press 1977.

INDEX

Academy of Political Science, 109
Adams, Charles K., 9
Adams, Herbert Baxter, 4, 8, 10, 11, 22, 119, 120
allgemeine Staatslehre, 13, 24, 25, 31, 63, 67, 145
American Academy of Political Science, 7
American Economic Association, 108, 110, 111
American Historical Association, 108, 110, 111
American Political Science Association, 1, 2, 4, 107–118, 147, 150; as a community of inquiry, 40; as an agent of social reform, 53, 54; early history of, 9, 10–11, 12; membership growth in, 12; presidents of, 8, 12
American Political Science Review, 7, 11, 112
American Social Science Association, 109
Aristotle, 63, 67
Ayer, A. J., 36

Bancroft, George, 6, 20, 21, 51
Bateman, Clifford R., 22
Beard, Charles A., 51–52, 76, 90, 91, 92
Becker, Carl, 84–85
behavioralism, 7, 149–150
Bentley, Arthur F., 126–129, 147
bicameralism, 91
Bluntschli, Johann K., 13, 23, 24, 25, 26, 27, 28, 121
Brown, Bernard, 27–28, 31
Bryce, James, 112, 115
Burgess, John W., 2, 3, 4, 10, 11, 13, 120, 147; and Columbia University, 6–7, 22, 51, 109; on the Constitution, 92, 93; on the Declaration of Independence, 76, 77; early career of, 5–6; and German political theory, 26, 27; in Germany, 21, 22, 34; on methodology, 119, 122, 124, 128; on national character, 29; on sovereignty 27, 28

cabinet government, 97, 99
checks and balances, 100, 146

163

About the Author

Dennis J. Mahoney is an attorney in private practice in California. He earned his Ph.D. in government from the Claremont Graduate University. He has taught at Claremont McKenna College, California State University, San Bernardino, and the University of La Verne College of Law; he is currently an adjunct faculty member in the department of law and public policy of the University of California, Riverside, Extension. He is the coeditor of three books: *The 1984 Election and the Future of American Politics* (with Peter Schramm); *The Framing and Ratification of the Constitution* (with Leonard W. Levy); and *The New Federalist Papers* (with J. Jackson Barlow and Thomas G. West).